Bremen compact
City guide

BECKS BISTRO

Lutz Liffers

Bremen compact

City guide

Edition Temmen

Aerial view on Bremens new »Überseestadt«

Bremen Highlights

1) Take hold of the Donkey's forefeet (page 24)
2) Enjoy the »Schlachte« with nice weather (page 43)
3) Discover the cultural heritage of mankind (page 25)
4) Visit three museums at once (page 63)
5) Drop some coins into the »Bremer hole« (page 8)
6) Tour the »Rosekeller« in the Ratskeller (Page 24)

In Brief

Bremen – The River-City

Bremen is about an hour's drive from the sea, yet sometimes as you walk through the old city center toward the Weser, you'll catch the scent of fresh sea air. Twice per day, **high tide** from the North Sea reaches the city and the waters of the rivers Weser, Lesum, Hunte and Wümme are pushed »backwards« towards land. After six hours the tide flows out again to the sea. This constant ebb and flow has created a natural environment, unique in Europe, on the coast of the North Sea. This environment, the Wattenmeer, influences life in Bremen to this day, as the phenomenon is important for the modern freight ships as they »ride« the wave of the tide all the way to the city harbor, bringing industrial goods, steel, cereals, feed grains, coffee, and much more.

The Weser has been the main artery of the city for hundreds of years. Early

Bremen's History in Brief…

780	Charlemagne sends Willehad to bring Christianity to Northern Germany. A church is built at the highest point in the city on the Bremer dune
888	Bremen attains the right to hold a public market
1358	Bremen joins the Hanseatic league
1522	Beginning of the Reformation in Bremen
1646	Bremen is recognized as a »Free City of the Empire«
1776	After U.S. independence, Bremen develops extensive trade contacts with North and South America
Starting 1870	The Weser is straightened. At Walle and Gröpelingen modern harbors are established. The A.G. Weser Shipyard also settles there
1944	Allied bombing destroys almost all barbor installations and many parts of the city
1945	April 27 – British troops liberate Bremen
1971	Founding of Bremen's university
1978	Daimler Benz begins production in Bremen
1996	Closure of Bremen's last great shipyard
2004	Bremen's City Hall and Roland are declared »World Heritage« monuments
2005	Bremen is named »City of Science«
2011	In the former warehouse and harbor area, the »Ubersee-stadt« is created – a new quarter to accommodate both residential and commercial properties.
2016	From May to October a new Weser ferry for pedestrians and cyclists operates from Überseestadt
2018	In no other German city do more people make their daily travels by bike
2019	A new city beach, »Waller Sand«, is being built in Überseestadt

on, fishermen settled on the shores and in the tributary of the Balge, where, it is thought, early inhabitants had a ford. During the 9th Century a small settlement grew here, and soon merchants came to trade. The »Schlachte« or what people in Bremen call the Weser Promenade, became a cosmopolitan harbor. In the early Middle Ages, the »Koggen« ships of the Hanseatic League came and went from this harbor, bringing wares from all over the globe. Later this harbor was the theater of much trade and passenger traffic to America. Immigrants shipping from Bremen brought considerable business to the city in those years.

... Bremen in Statistics

The land of Bremen covers a good 40,000 hecteres of land. It has nearly 681,000 residents and consists of two cities, Bremen and Bremerhaven. While Bremerhaven, at the mouth of the Weser, has become the center of Bremen's shipping industry – turning over some 73 million tons (as of 2015) – the City of Bremen distinguishes itself with brain power in the sciences and in the research and development departments of the large industrial establishments for automobiles and air and space travel. Because the city grew along the river, it is 38 kilometers long and only 16 kilometers wide. The good news is that you can be out in the beautiful landscape very quickly, even on a bike.

The Bremen Town Musicians at the west side of the City Hall

As always, Bremen lives from world trade – the great markets of China, India, Japan, Latin America or Eastern Europe have been important trading partners of Bremen merchants for a long time. Though today, if you are

Bremen under Water

If the Weser's flood tide brought the water mark to over 2.40 meters above the normal zero line, then large areas of the city would be under water. For this reason, Bremen is protected from the North Sea and the upper Weser by 155 kilometers of dike. The 40,000 square kilometers of area between the Werra and Aller rivers are especially subject to flood after heavy rainfall or a spring thaw, when the Weser alone is not sufficient to carry all of the water away. In 1981, there was a spectacular dike failure which led to the complete decimation of the extensive hobby gardens that had been cultivated in the overflow areas. Luckily, no lives were lost in the deluge.

The Roland

The so-called »Bremer Loch« collects money to support a public civil foundation. If you drop coins in there you hear the Bremen town musicians singing. Try to find - location next to the house of parlament

looking for the right freighter for your goods, you need to go to the container terminal in Bremerhaven or to the new Jade Weser Port in Wilhelmshaven. That is where the large (and ever larger) container ships are landing these days. This has left the former Bremen harbor area of the »Schlachte« free for three whole kilometers of promenade along the river, great for walking, biking, skating, jogging or just strolling. It is no wonder that, come summer, thousands will be relaxing in the beer gardens and restaurants, enjoying the beautiful views or walking along the wharf where historic ship replicas, tourist cruisers and yachts are moored.

Climate Change and Protection against High Water

For centuries, the incoming flood tides from the North Sea have challenged the citizens of Bremen. Again and again, floods raged through the area.
For this reason, at the beginning of the 12th Century, the citizens of Bremen had already begun consulting the experts. Dutch colonists moved into the area and systematically drained it, building dikes **to protect the area against flooding**. To this day approximately 100 kilmeters of dike protect the city, which otherwise, would be under water nearly everywhere, twice per day. Today, further drainage systems have been added, for any water that seeps into the city must be pumped out again over the dikes.
Because of these problems with flooding, Bremen is especially sensitive to the threat of global **climate change** and the rising water levels that are connected with it. In the coming decades, it is presumed, the dikes will need to be augmented by as much as one meter to stem the rising tide. This will be a tremendous economic and technical challenge.
Climate protection, accordingly, is an important topic in Bremen: here we have Marum, an internationally known oceanic and climate research center, and in Bremerhaven, Bremen's twin on the Lower Weser, scientists from all over the globe work at the world-renouned Alfred Wegener Institute. Finally, in Bremerhaven's **Klimahaus**, visitors can find out about the intricacies of the world's climate and how this affects our lives.

Furthermore, the use and promotion of renewable energy sources is also of central importance, finding broad consensus in the population. In the past decades, Bremen has become a center for **wind energy**, in which research and production facilities cooperate closely. Bremen is home to over 140 wind energy companies, increasingly off-shore, as well, which set the pace for the transition to renewable energy in Germany.
Even tidal power is now finally going to be of positive use: in 2008, construction on the biggest new tidal power plant in Germany started just up-river from Bremen's stadium. The **Weserkraftwerk** (power plant), built underground next to the river, has (since Winter 2011) already produced up to 42 million kilowatt hours per year – enough to supply 17,000 Bremen households. Thus, every year, this tidal power plant keeps 35,500 tons of CO2 out of the atmosphere. Per second, 220 square meters of water enter the turbines at a speed of up to eight meters per second. Technically, the power plant is a challenge. Ebb and flood tides produce widely fluctuating levels of power, and the plant can only function well thanks to a sophisticated equalization system.
However – and this is typical for Bremen – the Weserwehr power plant has also been made to function in harmony with the immediate environment. The Weser has always been an important transit for **migratory fish**, which must go upstream to lay their eggs. Of

View of the Weser

course, a power plant extending across the river would present an unsurmountable obstacle. Thus, an extensive system of water ramps has been provided to allow the many species of migratory fish safe access to their traditional nurseries upriver.

One of the ramps for migratory fish

Bremen smartens up

The 1970s already saw the opening of a unique, »reformed« university, the fundamental ideas of which – project-oriented studies, interdisciplinary studies, dismantling of professorial fiefdoms – are today touted by many an older prestigious university, as »innovative« on the educational marketplace. Since that time, Bremen has become an academically prominent location, with two universities, the various art and technical schools, and a highly developed research environment with many well-known institutes, including, for example, the German Center for Polar Research in Bremerhaven. In 2005, Bremen became the first city to be named »City of Science«.

Bremen Celebrates

Bremen presents itself best through its many festivals and cultural events. The traditional events and more recently established cultural events, many of which attract a younger crowd, all take their rightful places together in the celebration calendar.

The season starts with a bang, in the first days of January, with the **Sixdays** in the Convention Hall. This is the world's largest indoor bike race, since 1965. With live music, shows, loges for prominent guests, a beer garden, and »the biggest Kohl and Pinkel feast in the world,« amongst other food concessions, it actually resembles a country fair more than a sporting event. The racetrack is merely the center of this six-day event, which remains one of the most popular attractions in Northern Germany.

The **Schaffermahl** (Schaffer Feast) is one traditional winter event that most citizens and visitors must enjoy vicariously. Originally held to see Bremen's ship captains off on their long voyages, it is still strictly invitation only. Ever since 1545, the »brotherhood« and special guests have met on the second Friday in February to eat »stockfish« and cabbage and discreetly collect funds for »Haus Seefahrt,« the traditional seaman's charitable association.

The **Bremer Eiswette** (Ice Wager), which first took place in 1829, is a rollicking spectacle on the banks of the Weser. It is street theater on the Osterdeich, in which a featherweight tailor must attempt to cross the Weser to see whether it »stands« (steiht), ie., is frozen, or »goes« (geiht) and will be open for ships. Most prominent among the crowds of spectators are the »Three Wise Men,« seven »novices« in bowler hats, among others whose duties include recalling and satirizing the highs and lows of Bremen politics in the course of the year. Afterwards, 600 invited guests will take part in an exclusive feast.

The Weser Promenade at night

The Bremen Samba Carnival

At the beginning of February, the »Viertel« neighborhood heats up with the biggest **Samba Carnival Parade** in Germany. A thousand drummers, pipers, and anyone who wants to, can dress up (or down) and dance to hot South American rhythms or enjoy watching as the parade makes its colorful way from the marketplace into the Ostertor for a fun, carefree party.
In March, the siren song of the **Osterwiese** (Easter Meadows) with its wild rides and concessions, has nine days to lure you in. It is held on the Bürgerweide.
In the bordering conference center the international jazz scene gathers for **Jazzahead!** – a sort of Jazz specialist convention, each year focusing on a particular land. And, of course, you will always find a top-notch act on-stage while the luminaries of jazz meet.

The international literary festival **Poetry on the Road** is a similarly ambitious undertaking. Authors come from all over the world to blend the human voice with instrumental sounds – South African rhythms meet up with crackling Swiss word acrobatics, or you might enjoy a meeting of the sounds and minds of moody, poetic souls, the Irish and the East European. A further attraction for literature fans is the **globale° – Festival of German Global Literature**, in which primarily young authors of bi-cultural background take the stage to share works in the language of the new homeland – Germany.
During the summer, the open-air gatherings and festivals nearly overlap with each other. In the north, you are welcome again to the **Hafenfest Vegesack** (Harbor Festival), where fans of the maritime will feel especially at home enjoying a breath of fresh sea air in Germany's oldest, and recently remodelled, artificial harbor.
A very special event is the world-renowned street-circus festival **La Strada**. With 120 shows, 60 artists from 13 countries and a number of premier events, the festival can be counted among the most popular events for street-performers in Europe. Thousands come for a week of graceful acrobatics, clowning, and magnificent productions.
The **bremer shakespeare company** moves to the Bürgerpark during this time and stages its most beautiful productions against the romantic backdrop of the park. The culmination of the **Bremer Theater Sommer** (Bremen Summer Theater Festival) is always a great celebration feast served by the ensemble in the park.

Also in a park, but Knoops Park in St. Magnus (north Bremen), the German Chamber Philharmonic Orchestra plays the **Summer in Lesmona** festival amidst ancient trees, in romantic clearings and meadows. Most concert-goers bring blankets and picnic baskets filled with delicacies to pass the time. The three-day music festival enjoys cult status and represents a very special experience.

Since the summer of 2017, the district Hemelingen (Sporthafen Hemelingen) plays host to a fantastic festival: **DIE KOMPLETTE PALETTE**: Cool music, young culture, delicious drinks – outdoors, right on the bank of the Weser river.

In autumn proper comes the **Music Festival of Bremen**, bringing well-known classical musicians, soloists and ensembles, to the city's many excellent concert venues.

Yet for many, the high point of the year has to be October's **Freimarkt**, Germany's oldest fair. During these days, tens of thousands travel from all over Northern Germany to eat, drink, be merry, and go on wild rides.

Winter begins in Bremen's parks and suburbs with »lantern walks,« where groups of children carry colorful, sometimes home-made, lanterns as they sing with friends or school classes on a twilight walk. In the west of Bremen, in Gröpelingen, a unique festival of light and story-telling takes place. Thousands walk through the dark streets of this borough as part of the so-called **Feuerspuren** (Trail of Fire) – **the International Storytellers Festival**, in which story-tellers from across Europe come to tell stories at unusual locations in a variety of languages.

Roland decorated during the funfair FREIMARKT

In the last weeks before Christmas, you will find the **Christmas Market** on Bremen's historic Marktplatz and surrounding areas. This historic setting lends the event an aura that brings it into one league with the legendary Christmas Market of Nuremburg. Along with spiced wine and Christmas sweets, merchants and craftsmen offer their fine wares to passers-by. The **Schlachtezauber** takes place at the same time as the Christmas Market. There on the banks of the Weser, visitors enjoy the numerous concessions, including arts and crafts stands in the flavour of a market place of the Middle Ages.

Bremen Cooks

Betty Gleim (1781 – 1827), author, teacher, and women's rights activist, remarked in her well-known cookbook written in 1808, that »in Bremen, food is prepared in a unique and peculiar way«. In fact, the cuisine of Bremen is a unique combination of the farmhouse food of Lower Saxony and the no less hearty, down-to-earth dishes of the sailors who traveled the world for Bremen's merchants.

Eel, shrimps, matie, herring and stockfish provide a basis for Bremen's maritime cuisine, of which **Stockfish** (salted dried codfish and klipfish) above all was the staple in Bremen households. Today, only available in the best fish markets, stockfish is a delicacy to be rediscovered. For families that could not afford to eat fish from the sea, the river offered a rich dietary basis: crayfish, eel-pout, lamprey and Weser salmon. Today, all of these species are either extinct or under protection. Only the »stinkfish«, the **Stint**, a quick little predator the size of a finger, still swarms periodically after hatching in the river. Then as now, stint is a favorite – dusted in rye flour and fried in butter, served with lamb's lettuce or potato salad, it tastes wonderful.

Less well-known today is Bremen's traditional casserole dish, **Pfluckte Finken**, consisting of corned beef or pork, carrots, potatoes, and white beans. In earlier times, this hearty casserole was apparently served day after day on board Bremen's whalers. The sailors gave the dish its unusual name: »pflucken« is the skinning, gutting and cutting up of a whale and »Finken« were the leftover bits and pieces. The name of this dish, then, might be tersely translated as »chopped bits.«

A delicacy of Bremen: Kohl and Pinkel (Brown Cabbage)

However, the very heart of Bremen's cuisine hangs on the green cabbage. Originally from the areas around the Mediterranean, it now belongs to Northern Germany by long association. In Bremen, this very healthful, vitamin C-rich vegetable is also called **»Brown Cabbage«** and is prepared in a large variety of ways. One classic recipe includes brown cabbage simmered long and gently with duck or goose fat, salt and onions, then served with smoked pork chops (Kasseler), special »pinkel« sausages and boiled, glazed potatoes. The pinkel sausage, in general, contains various meat ingredients, groats and spices, yet each butcher has his own special and often secret recipe. The »pinkel« of Oldenburg and Rotenburg, for example, will taste fundamentally different from each other. The name comes from the origin of the sausage skin in a certain segment of the cow's intestine.

This is the meal associated with the Bremen tradition of the »Kohl and Pinkel« tour, in which a group of friends and acquaintances get together for a long walk along dikes, through frosty fields and woods, with a variety of games and a sip or two of schnapps to keep them warm along the way. Of course, the goal they are moving towards is crucial: a good, down-to-earth meal of brown cabbage, assorted meats, pinkel sausage and potatoes, all-you-can-eat, usually in a warm, comfortably rustic restaurant. Anyone who still needs dessert after such a meal will do well to have **»Bremer Rote Grütze«**, a tart and refreshing compote of mixed berries.

For sweets, you will find Bremer Bubber, Bremer Moppen, brown cake, pumpkin bread, pumpernickel pudding, and elderberry soup with rock candy, yet these play a subsidiary role in Bremen's cuisine and, for true dessert-lovers, these dishes may be either too sweet or not sweet enough. However, there is one sweet Christmas specialty that you simply should not miss: **Bremer Klaben**, a mighty stollen of citron, almonds, raisins, currants, cardamom, orange blossom, and just enough flour to hold it all together. It is served whole. You cut it in slices and enjoy it spread thinly with butter.

»Brown« Cabbage – Bremen's Green Vegetable

Citizens of Bremen not only have the »fifth season« that is Freimarkt time, we also have a a custom of »Kohl and Pinkel« a party that celebrates the so-called »brown« (actually green) cabbage of the region. This extremely healthful vegetable virtually dominates the cuisine of Bremen during the »kohl and pinkel« season – that is, all winter. During this frosty time, all over Bremen and environs, you will see groups of varying size enjoying a long walk along the dikes before ending up at a restaurant specializing in »kohl and pinkel« the traditional »brown« cabbage meal. On the long walk, many indulge in a round of traditional Frisian »Bosseln« a kind of ballgame. Watch out drivers and bikers! Balls have been known to fly astray.

Werder Bremen – Green-White For Life

SV Werder Bremen is a football club with a long tradition and history that only few clubs in Germany can match. The club was founded on February 4th, 1899 by a group of young people who played their first games on the Stadtwerder. Today, Werder Bremen counts 37,000 members and, in addition to football, features athletics, gymnastics, table tennis, handball and chess – which is rarely to be found in today's Bundesliga landscape. A special feature of the club is its social commitment. Under the brand name **»Werder bewegt - Lebenslang« (Werder Moves – For Life)**, Werder runs numerous projects that focus on issues beyond the Hanseatic city's borders, such as inclusion, tolerance, health or environmental awareness and sustainability. Werder is a leader in implementing corporate social responsibility (CSR).

For decades, fans have very strongly identified with the club. This turns the city green and white – the clubs colors – on match days. Werder fans are extremely loyal to their club – through the good times and the bad. This euphoria and love for their club is not uncommonly expressed in form of fan campaigns which regularly gain nationwide recognition.

In the »eternal« Bundesliga table, Werder Bremen takes second place behind only FC Bayern Munich, making it one of the most successful German football clubs. After the first championship in 1965, great success followed under coach Otto Rehhagel in the early 1980s. After brief relegation and return to the 1. Bundesliga, the team immediately achieved 30 wins. Between 1982 and 1987, the team continuously qualified for the UEFA Cup. In 1992, the team won the UEFA Cup Winners' Cup, and in 1993 the German Championship. After 14 successful years, coach Otto Rehhagel retired from the club in 1995. Various coaching changes followed, with rather mediocre placements in the Bundesliga table. In 1998/99, Werder Bremen found itself at the bottom of the table, but was able to re-build to play top-level football under coach Thomas Schaaf, winning the DFB Pokal in 1999. In the 2003/04 season, the team secured both the championship title and DFB Pokal – the so-called »Double« – and Werder again won the DFB Pokal in 2009.

Werder's story and history has been marked by many great players – i.e. Rudi Völler, Johan Micoud, Diego, Ailton and the legendary Claudio Pi-

The only football stadium in Germany that can be reached by boat

zarro. However, Werder's philosophy also includes the promotion of young talents such as Mesut Özil or current players Maximilian and Johannes Eggestein. After a few years of struggle against relegation in the early 2010s, the young head coach Florian Kohfeldt seems to have successfully turned the team around. Werder is Bremen and Bremen is Werder. This becomes clear in many places in the city, most of all the the **»Weser Stadium«**, which lies in the middle of the city »where the Weser makes a big turn«. If you want to experience a unique football atmosphere up close, you can do so in one of the pubs in the Viertel or around the stadium (for example, on Brommyplatz, in the »Taubenschlag«). To dive deeper into Werder's history, go to the "Wuseum" or book a stadium tour.

Wuseum - Werder Bremen Museum, Franz-Böhmert-Straße 1c, Tel. 434594350, Tue-Fri Noon-5pm (Jan-Feb 12-3pm), Sat-Sun + public holidays 12-3pm; Open on home match days, 3 hours to 1 hour before kickoff.
www.werder.de

Johannes Eichwede

Werder Bremen Fans celebrates the »Double«. (2004)

Pannekoekschip

City Tours

Tour 1
In Bremen's Living room – Marktplatz, City Hall, and Cathedral

In Bremen, the **Marktplatz** (marketplace) is often called the city's »living room,« and in fact, it is a place to feel at home. Anyone with a free minute loves to sit before the impressive backdrop of the historic facades on the west side, enjoying the sun Meanwhile, musicians may have taken up their posts in front of the Roland statue, and under the arcade of the City Hall, a tired shopper or a parent surrounded by noisy kids might stop for a quick rest before rejoining the crowds in the stores of Sögestraße or Obernstraße. On these stone benches under the **arcade**, Bremen's citizens have sat through the ages, watching the comings and goings on the Marktplatz. Long ago, officials sat on the benches in Roland's shadow to regulate weights and measures, and from the cathedral to the Schütting (guildhall), to the City Hall (Rathaus), the »cabbage peddlers«, would cry out their wares, or farmers selling cattle, swine, oxen or fowl, would do their business.

The Marktplatz is still the center of Bremen's public life today. There you will find the **»miniature Freimarkt«** for the very young or the beautiful **Christmas Market**, or even a gathering of Werder Bremen soccer fans celebrating after an important game or title. The Marktplatz is also the frequent goal of political demonstrations, because, from Bremen's twin seats of government, the City Hall and **Bremen's State Government building**, the politicians can't help but see all the people.

The hallmark of Bremen is the mighty statue of **Roland** (1), three meters high, erected in 1404. Though many other medieval cities chose this faithful servant of Charlemagne as the symbol of their independence, Bremen's stone statue is the oldest and the largest. He stands confidently facing the **cathedral** (Dom), which, until the 16th century, housed the independent citizenry's most powerful opponent, the ducal bishop. On Roland's golden coat of arms is Bremen's declaration of independence:

Vryheit do ik iu openbar
De karl und menich vorst vorwar
Desser stede ghegheven hat
Des danket gode is min radt.
(Freedom do I embody for you
That Charlemagne and many a prince, it's true,
Have given to this place.
Thank God for it, is my advice.)

The powerful Bremen merchants never again wanted to be under church or aristocratic domination, and thus emphasized their sole obedience to the emperor. However, asserting that Charlemagne had already declared Bremen independent was a well-calculated bluff. It was only in 1646, after quietly paying a large bribe, that Bremen was declared a Free City of the Empire, according to the **Linzer Diploma** of Emperor Ferdinand III.

If you are facing Roland, turn now to the **City Hall** (2) on your right for a

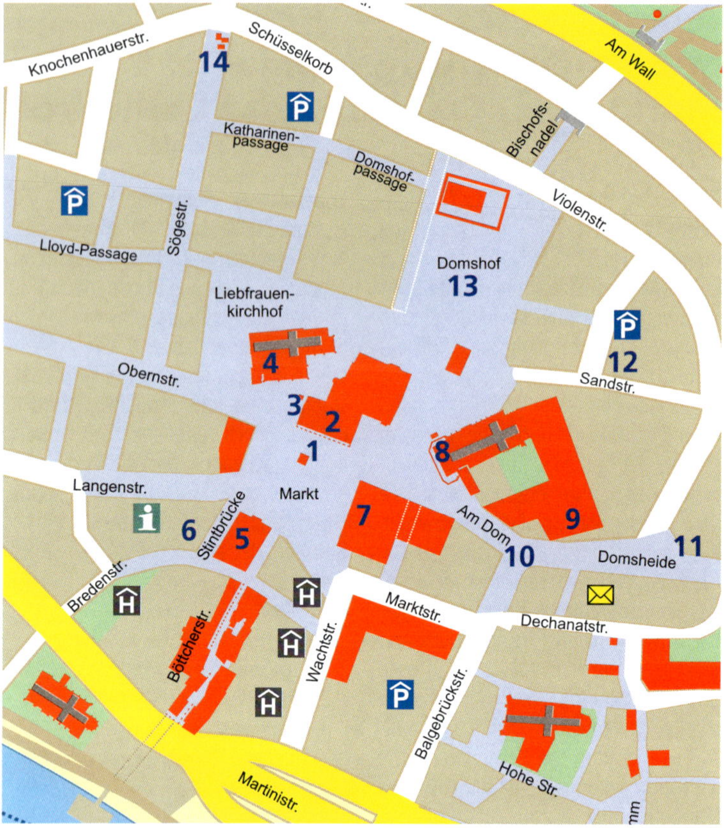

1 Roland
2 Rathaus (City Hall)
3 Bremer Stadtmusikanten
4 Unser Lieben Frauen
5 Schütting
6 Kontorhaus
7 Haus der Bürgerschaft
8 St. Petri-Dom (Cathedral)
9 Glocke
10 Domsheide
11 Land- und Amtsgericht
12 Haus der Wissenschaft
13 Domshof
14 Schweinedenkmal

view of one of the most beautiful Renaissance facades in Northern Europe. At the climax of Bremen's might as a Hanseatic city, between 1605 and 1616, master builder Lüder von Bentheim reconstituted the severe Gothic facade from 1400, creating the present richly figural facade you see today.
He added the great central bay window, the magnificent gables and the arcade to give the building a new face that would better reflect Bremen's growing significance. The figures over the arcade are an eloquent statement of the Calvinistic merchants' values:

The Bremen City Hall is a masterpiece of the Weser Renaissance

the image of a corrupt Catholic church may be seen in the crawling pope, ridden by a beautiful woman, symbol of worldly power. Or, at another point, the female allegory of temperance and self-discipline thins the wine with water.
However, more local symbolism also finds a place in the depictions. The figure of a woman protectively holding her chicks has been interpreted as an image of Bremen's founding legend in which, during a terrible storm, a beleaguered tribe of settlers saw a moorhen taking refuge with her chicks on the high ground of a dune. Seeing that this was a safe place, they took the creature's example and fled to the high ground that would become the site of Bremen's first settlement.
Above the balcony stand eight large staTue representing Charlemagne and his seven archdukes. This is yet another indication of Bremen's loyalty to the ideal of the free imperial city, however far this might yet have been from reality. On the sides are figures from the Old and New Testaments. The inscriptions, which refer to Classical philosophers, were added later.
Next, find the door of the **Lower City Hall** – it is almost always open. After the decorative exuberance of the facade, you will find a stark contrast in the severe Gothic style which has been retained here in the original. In former times, a part of this area was the lower court of law, while other parts served as an extension of the market place. Today the Lower Hall is used for artistic or cultural exhibitions and is generally open to all.
The magnificent **Upper Hall** presents further symbolic figuration of medieval Bremen's might. This hall, 40 meters long and 13 meters wide, is used now for important receptions and debates organized by the president of the senate or senatorial colleagues. Painted medallions of German emperors from Charlemagne to Sigismund decorate the exposed wooden beams and shining brass chandeliers

The »Güldenkammer« on the upper floor of the City Hall

bring a warm glow to the room. Also hanging from the ceiling are intricate models of historic warships. In earlier times, their miniature canons would be loaded with a small charge of gun powder and set off at the climax of a state banquet or in honor of a special guest. The Upper Hall is also the scene of the annual »Schaffer Feast«, a charitable gathering to benefit Bremen's seafaring folk. The feast has a tradition extending back to the 16th century.

In the Upper Hall, a mural depicts Charlemagne and Bishop Willehad as the founders of the city. A second mural entitled »The Judgment of Solomon« served to remind magistrates that true justice is the ultimate goal of law.

One of the City Hall's special treasures is the **»Güldenkammer«** the room inside of the central bay window, in which the city councilmen could conduct confidential business. The upper floor presumably had been used as the podium for the council's chapel, ever since the Middle Ages. Here, too, those working at the City Hall would be reminded in allegory and classical reference of the fundamental duties of good government. After years of neglect, in 1903, the derelict room was transformed into a Jugendstyl masterpiece by the Worpswede artist Heinrich Vogeler. The gold and leather wall-coverings, ornamented paneling, chandeliers, fireplaces, even the door handles, are all designed to harmonize in the graceful loops and curves of German Art Nouveau.

City Hall Tours

Mon–Sat at 16:00, Sun 12:00.
(changes possible, no tours possible at senate receptions or events, for further information please contact

the BTZ), duration approx. 1 hour. Meeting point at the Town Hall entrance nearest the Cathedral, next to the statue of the knight on horseback (small door on the left, next to the display case).
Bookings via Bremer Touristik-Zentrale (BTZ), Tel. 3080010
www.rathaus.bremen.de/rathaus/rathausfuehrungen

The Ratskeller

The Ratskeller is the »delectable foundation,« as medieval contemporaries called it, of Bremen's City Hall. Since 1405, the **Ratskeller** has had the right to sell and serve the council's wine. Heinrich Heine praised Bremen's Ratskeller in his poem »In the Harbor.« In 1827, the poet Wilhelm Hauff wove his surrealist fantasy about love, death, and politics around its dim alcoves. In his more sober prose, the young Friedrich Engels would fondly recall tipsy evenings there.

The tri-partite Gothic main hall is still a scene of pleasant, relaxed sociability. Guests and natives alike sit at the long oak tables, surrounded by the picturesque, huge (now empty) barrels built into the walls. Across from these are the »Priölken« (alcoves) in which merchants, after long negotiation, might seal a bargain. The wooden doors of these alcoves were not closed, ostensibly to demonstrate the honorable status of the business.

Guests may choose from among 600 of the best wines from thirteen German wine areas. But don't worry – if you only want a glass or a carafe, you will easily find something you will like on the shorter list of open wines. Tasty

The traditional »Schaffermahl« takes place annually in the City Hall

hors d'oeuvres and small meals are also available.

But the actual kingdom of cellar-master Karl-Josef Krötz and his employees

UNESCO-World Cultural Heritage sites

Bremen's Roland and City Hall are unique witnesses for the evolution of the political autonomy and commercial rights of the European middle classes. These two objects are emblematic for the development of the Hanseatic League to a mighty federation of nearly autonomous city states within the Holy Roman Empire. For this reason, in 2004, UNESCO put Bremen's Roland and City Hall onto the list of World Cultural Heritage sites that are under their special protection.

The Apostle cellar with very old wine barrels, the oldest from 1653

begins beyond the comfortable room described above. Next to the main cellar area lies the **Hauffkeller**, so called because of artist Max Slevogt's various colorful murals inspired by Hauff's novella Fantasies in the Bremen Ratskeller. In the adjoining Apostle and Rose Cellars, very old barrel wines are stored, among them a **Rüdesheim Apostle Wine** from 1727, supposedly the oldest still drinkable wine in Germany. In the Rose Cellar is the oldest wine of all from 1653, another Rüdesheimer – a priceless vintage, but one whose flavor has yet to be sampled. Beyond this, from the Liebfrauen Church to the cathedral, stretch kilometers of subterranean storage alcoves, in which Herr Krötz has carefully stored up to 500,000 bottles to age as they should. From here, connoisseurs of German wines the world over, including many ambassadors, order their wines. Since 2002, Bremen even has its own vineyard – Cellar master Krötz leases an 850 square meter tract of prime agricultural land on the Mosel »Erdener Treppchen«, yielding grapes for the highest quality sweet wines.

Bremen's Ratskeller

Though a seat at one of the long tables will usually be available, if you want to have a »Priölke« you will need to reserve ahead of time. Tel. 321676, daily from 11am to midnight. Tours of the Ratskeller may be booked over the Bremer Touristik Zentrale, January to mid-November, Fri. 4pm. March to October, in addition, 3pm (except Fridays). Groups may negotiate special tours. Meeting place: Tourist Information Böttcherstraße 4/ Marktplatz. Tel. 3080010. At the back oft he City Hall is a small store in which Ratskeller wines are sold. Open Mon – Fri. 9am – 6pm, Sat. 9.30am – 3pm, www.ratskeller.de

On the Marktplatz

Gerhard Marcks' group of figures representing the **Bremer Stadtmusikanten** (3), Bremen Town Musicians, created in 1953, is a modern masterpiece of formal clarity. No matter that the Grimm Brothers' musicians never actually got to Bremen, but found their cozy house outside of the city walls – the sculpture recalls the animals' plight and we rejoice in the home they did find. It is said that anyone who grips the donkey's front hooves and makes a wish, will have his wish come true.

On the west side of City Hall you will also find the **Church of Unser Lieben Frauen** (4), also called Liebfrauen Church, of which the north nave and crypt were built in the 11th century. Originally, this oldest parish church in Bremen was dedicated to Saint Vitus. The crypt of the 1020 A.D. building is still preserved. Second to the bishop's cathedral, this was considered the most important sacred architecture in Bremen. It served the city council as a place of worship and was later used as a military chapel. Alfred Manessier's beautiful modern windows shed a colorful light on the consecrated room.

Across from City Hall, you will find the **Schütting** (5), traditional seat of the Merchants' Guild. An old Merian engraving of the Marktplatz shows the Schütting as significantly larger than the City Hall, and in fact, for many centuries, it was the actual center of power in the city. The destinies of Bremen's affairs and of many citizens lay in the hands of the influential Elderleute, the spokesmen for the merchants, who maintained a worldwide network of trade relations and brought wealth and prosperity to Bremen.

At the height of their power, around 1537, the merchants entrusted Johann de Buschener of Flanders with the task of designing a Renaissance palace that would overshadow the

The mighty towers of the cathedral, the parlament and the city hall at the Marktplatz

View of Schütting (chamber of commerce), rebuild after the war

(then) plain Gothic style of City Hall. Yet from this magnificence, only the east gable remains – the rest of the facade was later renovated in Baroque style, and the grand stairway and entrance were added in the 19th century. At that time, the merchants' chosen motto was carved over the portals, **»Buten und Binnen, Wagen und winnen«** or »Abroad and within – Dare and win!«

Various merchant coats of arms are also represented on the facade. If you look carefully, you will see one of these, with fish on it, belonging to one of the oldest merchant groups of Bremen, the Bergenfahrer, whose trade in stockfish – dried codfish – and herring from Scandinavia laid the foundation for Bremen's wealth. Right next door to the Schütting, the **Kontorhaus am Markt** (6) was originally built for the Berliner Disconto Bank between 1910 and 1912. In 2002, it was hollowed out to the exterior walls and completely redesigned as a modern shopping mall with a beautiful atrium at its core. At the re-opening festivities in 2003, Bremen Investment Company managers spoke of a »hint of Milan« adding grace to the elegant offices, bistros and boutiques, and inviting us to relax and enjoy the beautiful things and gourmet food offered there. On the east side of the Marktplatz, you will find the modern **Haus der Bürgerschaft** (7), the seat of Bremen's state government. At the beginning of the 1960s, Wassili Luckhart »old master of the modern« won the contract to design this house of parliament. His brave plan – for a glass cube that would nonetheless harmonize respectfully with the medieval buildings already on the square – was quite controversial. It was the current conservative Bürgerschaft President Hagedorn who spoke vehemently for the modern building.

His argument: we can't cover up the wounds of war with imitation medieval facades. Bremen needs a modern parliamentary building that will reflect the new democratic beginnings after 1945.

Luckhart's architecture is not only a self-confident symbol for transparency and aesthetic values on the exterior, inside, too, the space allows for a congenial interaction of functionality and beauty. The **auditorium** at the heart of the building is especially inviting for discussion, and visitors sit in low balconies that put them practically into the middle of the action.

This »front and center« atmosphere of politics is self-evident in Bremen. The Marktplatz, forming a wideopen center directly bordered by the City Hall and the House of the Bürgerschaft (Citizenry), is the goal of many a demonstration. Meanwhile, on any normal workday, you might see senators arriving on foot or bike, or hurrying across the square to their next appointment.

In 2005 a small **sculpture garden** was opened to the right of the main entrance for the sculptures of Gerhard Marcks, that were made by the sculptor at the time of origin of the Parliament. In the building further works are displayed: "Tatenlos" (Deedless) and "Mädchen mit großem Tuch" (Girl with a big cloth) are loans from the Gerhard Marcks House. (see page 70).

Behind the House of the Bürgerschaft are the remains of a neo-Gothic construction that once held the stock exchange (Börsenhof). In 2001, this building was reconstructed to house administrative offices of the state government. Between the stock exchange and the Luckhard building stands the »Fleischwolfbrunnen« (Meat-mincers' Fountain), an ironic memento mori from the sculptor and artist Daniel Spoerri, born in 1930.

Haus der Bürgerschaft

Tours are offered at times that the parliament is not in session. Regular exhibitions, mostly on historical topics, are held in the foyer or reception hall.

The elegant »Kontorhaus« next to Marktplatz

St. Petri Dom

From the steps of the **St. Petri Cathedral** (8) you can clearly see the slope down to the Marktplatz. The cathedral was built at the highest point of the dune on which, in the 8th century, the first settlers had taken refuge from the untamed waters of the Weser and the North Sea and built their small fishing and trading village. In 780, when Charlemagne directed the priest Willehad to establish a bishop's seat in Bremen, his interest lay in securing and extending the uncertain northern borders of his empire. When the Archbishop Ansgar was compelled by the Norsemen to flee a Hamburg in flames, his asylum in Bremen brought the city the status of an archbishopric and made it a center of missionary activities in Northern Europe.

There is nothing left of the wooden structure that Willehad built. It is the Romanesque basilica from the 11th century that has withstood war and fire and now constitutes the oldest part of the cathedral. In 1250, building was resumed in Gothic style. In 1482, the north nave and tower were seriously damaged by fire, and in 1522, with the unrest of the Reformation, the Catholic bishop was expelled and the cathedral was plundered and closed down. By 1638, when the south tower collapsed, the cathedral was practically a ruin.

It was only in the late 19 century that prosperous citizens began to see a cultural inheritance worth retaining in the cathedral. Starting in 1888, Max Salzmann undertook a comprehensive restoration. The towers were raised to 98 meters and the facade was redesigned in neo-Gothic style.

Charlemagne (with the face of Wilhelm II) as founder of the bishopric of Bremen

That the cathedral's facade was born of the 19th century sensibilities is betrayed by the central of five **figures** placed between the arching portals. This figure is supposed to represent Charlemagne as founder of the bishop's seat, yet his features resemble those of Kaiser Wilhelm II.

The bronze doors, created by Peter Fuchs in 1898, depict scenes from the New Testament. Just beyond the entrance on your right is a spiral staircase, consisting of 265 steps, leading up to the **south tower**. For a small fee, you can climb to the top for a wonderful view of the entire city.

The Cathedral's interior consists of three large galleries. The sandstone pillars were recently repainted in what art historians believe to be authentic colors – gold and warm pastels, which give the space a pleasant, comfortable atmosphere. Meanwhile, the stylistic differences among the three long gal-

View into the choir of the Bremen cathedral

leries are remarkable. While the south nave surrounds the visitor with the heaviness of the pure Romanesque style, the **Gothic north nave**, reconstructed in 1482 after a devastating fire, stretches seemingly heavenward on seemingly delicate, filigree arches. The great mid-section, in Romanesque style with Gothic overlay, offers views towards the choir and altar, then back to the balcony where the tri-manuel **Sauer Organ** (A) in late Romantic style, from 1894, is enthroned. Despite their differences, the three ships of the cathedral form an impressively harmonious unity.

Many of the cathedral's artworks bear witness to the conflict between Bremen's Calvinistic citizenry and the church as a last bastion of Catholicism. For example, sculptor Jürgen Kriebel's richly-carved **pulpit** (B) in the middle nave, from 1641, demonstratively rejects the unadorned style of the Calvinistic majority. One particularly valuable decorative piece is the **Lettnerbrüstung** (C) on the balcony, created around 1500 by a family of artists which had come to Bremen from Brabant. The carving depicts an important juncture in the city's history: Charlemagne and Willehad are seen, flanked by city and church officials, holding a model of the cathedral.

The **carved wings of the choir seating** (D) are another of the important artworks remaining in the cathedral. Nearly demolished in 1823 when the seating was renovated, these carvings were saved and mounted in the south nave. Here Bremen's history also surfaces in the depiction of Old Testament scenes: one of these brings up the bitter conflict between the archbishop and the city, which - according to the legend - led to the destruction of the first wooden Roland in 1366. Many of the richly decorated grave plaques are part of the Lutheran history of the building. The gravestone of the Freiherr von Knigge (1752–1796), well-known for his sharp wit and theater criticism, and famous in Germany for his humanistic and rational precepts for good manners, may also be found there.

Be sure not to miss the cathedral's **crypts**. Fans of Romanesque architecture will enjoy the capitals (circa 1100) in the east crypt, on which pagan and Christian figures mingle. The west crypt is dominated by three 13th century bronze baptismal fonts on lion pedestals. The oldest stone sculpture of the cathedral is also to be found in the west crypt: a figure of Christ enthroned on the world. In the west crypt lies another treasure: an organ built by Gottfried Silbermann in Freiberg, Saxony in 1732. Following Germany's reunification in 1989 the Silbermann Museum in Dresden produced a copy of the valuable instrument.

In the south cross-nave you will find the **Dom-Museum** (Cathedral's Museum), where valuable historical artifacts concerning the cathedral,

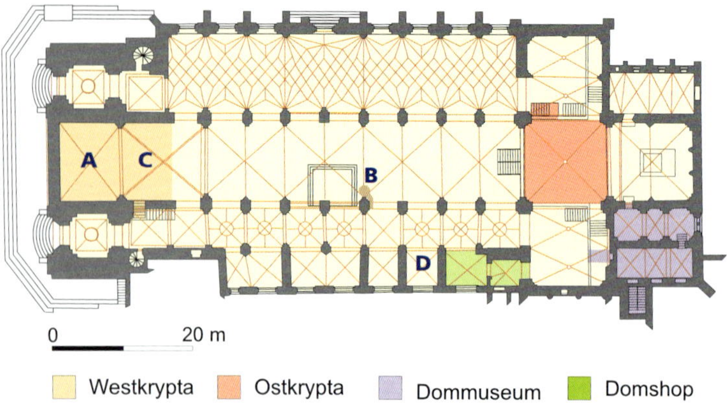

found when archeological work was undertaken in the 1970s, are on exhibition. Especially interesting are the robes, gold artifacts, and other objects from the various tombs. You will also find vivid historical documentation of the cathedral, from the first wooden construction to the art historical reconstructions of the late 19th century. In the direct vicinity of the cathedral is the **Bleikeller** (Lead Cellar), a somewhat controversial attraction. It contains eight mummies collected more or less by chance over the centuries. The first corpse, from the 15th century, was a roofer who died in a fall at work. He was brought to the Bleikeller and forgotten there. The extreme dryness of the rooms eventually mummified the body, which was only rediscovered many years later. However, after the marvelous mummifying effects of the Bleikeller had been recognized, the place was used to store anybody who died without relations to claim them. Though by the early 19th century this form of »burial« had been forbidden, the Romanticists, satisfying a neo-Gothic appetite for horror, made the Bleikeller a tourist attraction. The eight mummies there are still on exhibition.

In the former courtyard of the cathedral you will find the **Bremen Bible Garden**, in which over 60 different medicinal herbs are cultivated. Created in 1998, it is a peaceful refuge in the heart of the hectic city. The garden features a statue remembering the pilgrims of the »Jacobs Way.« During the Middle Ages, Bremen was a station on this popular route from Scandinavia, through Southern France, to Santiago de Compostela

Pilgrim statue in the »bible garden«

in Northern Spain. Once per month during the summer, a botanical tour of the garden takes place. No reservation is necessary.

(Contact »Bible gardener« pastor.fluegger@stpetridom.de)

St. Petri Dom

Mon–Fri. 10am–5pm, Sat 10am–2pm, Sun. 2pm–5pm, during the summer they stay open an hour longer, www.stpetridom.de

Ascent to the Tower

April, May, Oct. Mon–Fri 10am–4.30pm, Sat 10am–1.30pm, Sun 2pm–4.30pm; June–Sept. an hour longer on all days (265 steps)

Dom-Museum

Mon–Fri. 10am–4.45pm, Sat 10am–1.30pm, Sun. 2pm–4.45pm, Admission free

Communion plate and collection bag in the cathedral museum

Bleikeller
April, May, October:
Wed–Fri 10am–4.45pm, Sat 10am–4.45pm, Sun 12pm–4.45pm
June–Sept:
Mon–Fri 10am–5.45pm, Sat 10am–1.45pm,
Sun 12pm–5.45
Tours take place at variable times, depending on the season, www.stpetridom.de

Domsheide and Domshof

The **Glocke Concert Hall** (9) is directly connected to the Chapter House (Kapitelhaus). The octagonal floor plan of the medieval building originally located here was such that people had traditionally called it the »Glocke« or »Bell«. However, the Art Deco style concert hall was built by Walter Goering in 1928 and quickly became popular for its excellent acoustics. The Glocke was carefully restored and modernized just a few years ago, and has now resumed its series of ambitious concerts.

Die Glocke Concert Hall
Domsheide 6–8, Ticket-Service and info hotline: Tel. 336699, Mon–Fri 10am–6pm, Sat 10am–3pm, www.glocke.de
D'Oro café and restaurant in the Glocke (with a terrace in Domgarten), Tel. 3366888, opens 2 hours before events, kitchen open until 1 hour after the events

View into the main hall (Großer Saal) of the Glocke

The old main post office

The area in front of the Glocke Concert Hall is one of the main streetcar/bus junctions within Bremen, serving the stop **Domsheide** (10), pronounced, »Dome's Heide«. From here you can get to the main train station (5 min.), airport (15 min.), university, or just about anywhere in the city, very quickly.

»Domsheide« was named thus because the bishop used this place for public judgments of ecclesiastical law. A court of law may still be found here: the east side of the square is occupied by the **Land- und Amtsgericht** (11) (Land and Administrative Court), built by the Oldenburg architects Klingenberg and Weber from 1892 to 1895. The weighty facade depicting the ten commandments, makes the building easy to identify. During the dark history of the Nazi regime, this building was the scene of a 16-year old Polish boy's condemnation to death: hoping for the punishment of being sent home, the forced laborer Walerjan Wrobel had set a barn on fire. Yet another massive building in the pseudo-Gothic style of the 19th century is the **main post office** (Hauptpost), with its little Glockenspiel in a decorative gable.

From Domsheide, enter Violenstraße and Sandstraße to get to the house of the **Haus der Wissenschaft** (12), roughly translated, »House of the Sciences.« This humble citizen's house, now amidst a

Centrally located, the »Glocke« concert hall

The »Spitting Stone« on the outer courtyard of the cathedral marks the place at which the notorious19th Century murderess Gesche Gottfried, was executed

jumble of post-war buildings, was originally the Verein »Vorwärts« (Progress Club), founded in 1846 by the cigar-makers trade association to improve the general education of its members. At Sandstraße 5, writing, arithmetic, German, English, music, and sports were taught – and political activities were expressly prohibited. In 2005, this richly traditional house opened as the Haus der Wissenschaft, offering fascinating insights into the world of research and science. The universities, technical schools, and research institutes of Bremen present exhibitions and discussion groups on current topics. Every Saturday at 11am a brief lecture is given.
www.hausderwissenschaft.de

A few steps further along this street and you will reach the end of your mini tour of the heart of Bremen. In former times, not Domsheide but **Domshof** (13), to the north side of the cathedral, was the busy center of traffic for the city: carts waited here, travel and post carriages to the next large cities, and all of Bremen's major hotels were on this square. Furthermore, then as now, the square was the site of various markets. Today, numerous grocers, butchers, bakers, and a host of specialty food vendors are open for business daily in the shadow of the cathedral's spires, making this one of the largest and most picturesque open markets among the many in Bremen.
The **Neptune Fountain**, a playful creation by Waldemar Otto, shows a modern god as if just emerged from the waves, his sea horses spraying from their nostrils, while water nymphs and other mythical creatures gambol in the turbulent spume around him. On hot summer days, many a weary foot has found relief in the cool waters.
Near the fountain is the **»Spuckstein«**, a plaque recalling a gruesome incident in Bremen's history. There, on April 21, 1831, Gesche Gottfried, a murderess convicted of poisoning 15 people, including many of her family, was beheaded. In her testimony, she is said to have admitted, »I really loved doing evil«. The case had such notoriety that as many as 35,000 people gathered to see her execution. The »Spuckstein«, is so-called because for some ten years afterwards, people still went out of their way to spit on the commemorative stone in disgust.

The poison of Gesche Gottfried:
Themed walking tour through the city center in the footsteps of the mysterious murderess. The legendary Bremen poisoner keeps historians, psychologists, writers and film directors fully occupied. The tour through the historic city center follows in Gesche's footsteps; it recalls Gesche Gottfried's life as well as everyday life in Bremen during the early Biedermeier period.

The spray of the Neptune Fountain is refreshing on a hot summer's day

The huge sandstone edifices of various bank buildings now surround the square. The former Bremer Bank building, built in the Weser Renaissance style in the early 20th century, the 1891 Deutsche Bank building and the Bremer Landesbank – redesigned in brick expressionism by the London architecture firm Caruso St. John in 2016 – give the square a metropolitan feel. Opposite the Deutsche Bank is the entrance to **Markthalle 8**, also opened in 2016: In the tradition of classic market halls, select regional manufacturers present their food, dishes and other home-made products. The Deutsche Bank building has now been remodeled into the **Domshofpassage**, a shopping mall that will put you onto the path of some of the most elegant boutiques and chic bistros in Bremen: Domshofpassage, Katharinenpassage, then to the open pedestrian zone of Sögestraße. The end of the Sögestraße is marked by the **Schweinestatue**(14), a bronze statue of a herder with a group of pigs. The statue is a reference to the street's history, as it used to be a common route for driving pigs to the pasture in earlier times (Söge = Sau (sow) in Low German).

At 135 meters long by 60 meters wide, the Domshof is the largest square in Bremen, and, when unoccupied by the vendors, it could seem awfully empty. Thus, its size was seen as something of a problem for city planners. However, the problem was solved when **Café Alex**, an unabashedly modern glass cube, was built on the north side of the square. From the covered terrace on top you have a fantastic view of the Domshof and the cathedral.

BÖTTCHERSTRASSE

Tour 2
Along the Weser – Böttcherstraße, Weser Promenade, Media District and Teerhof

Böttcherstraße

A small alleyway to the left of the Schütting will lead you directly to Böttcherstraße (A), marked by a large, gilded bas-relief created by Bernhard Hoetger, entitled **»The Lightbringer«** (Der Lichtbringer). As you enter the street beneath the archway, expect a unique historical and architectural ensemble.

Böttcherstraße was originally the area where the barrel-makers serving the harbor lived. However, when the harbor moved further downstream, so did the coopers. The street fell into disrepair. In 1902, **Ludwig Roselius**, wealthy owner of Kaffee HAG, bought Böttcherstraße 6, an old packing house, which is the one remaining house of the original Böttcher Street. Then one after the next, he bought the other houses and had them demolished. The new west side of the street he had Alfred Runge and Eduard Scotland construct in so-called »Heimatschutzstil« (homeland style), using the traditional building materials of Lower Saxony and quoting from architecture of the Middle Ages. The opposite side of the street he handed over to **Bernhard Hoetger** to design. Approaching his task more as a sculptor than as an architect, Hoetger created a passionate expressionist landscape of facades, executed with the at that time most modern materials of the day – colored glass and steel, as well as traditional materials such as brick. Böttcherstraße remains a peerless example of its kind.

The sculpted, nearly organic, forms of the **Paula Becker-Modersohn Haus** (1) will give you a most vivid impression of the style. Like a cave, the dim foyer contains the stairs up to the exhibition rooms of the Kunstschau (Art Show). If you go through this foyer, past Hoetger's sculpture, »Madonna«, you will reach the **Handwerkerhof** (2) »Craftmen's Courtyard«, where you can buy original sweets from the Bremer Bonbonfabrik – the lollipops, hard candy and bonbons are produced on the spot.

Bremer Bonbonmanufaktur on Böttcher Street
Böttcherstr. 8, Tel. 36491231,
Mon–Sat 11am–6pm, April–Dec also
Sun. 12pm–5pm. Workshops at the
Schnoor-Shop, Tel 2342722

A bust of Ludwig Roselius commemorates his essential part in the project, and a fountain entitled »The Seven Lazy Brothers« gives form to one of Bremen's most beloved legends.

The Kunstschau itself houses an important collection of Worpswede artist **Paula Modersohn-Becker** (1876–1907), who became a pioneer of Modernism after her stay in Paris at the beginning of the 20th century. In Bremen and Worpswede she remained unrecognized: her paintings were at best »naive« according to the influ-

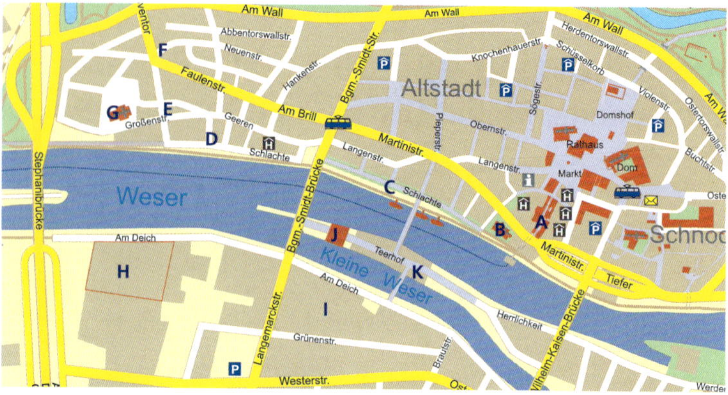

A	**Böttcherstraße**
B	**St. Martini**
C	**Schlachte**
D	**Youth hostel**
E	**Radio Bremen**
F	**Bamberger House**
G	**St. Stephani church**
H	**Beck's and Haake-Beck Visitor Center**
I	**Haus am Deich**
J	**Weserburg Museum / GAK**
K	**Teerhof**

ential artist Arthur Fitger, who wrote a damning review of one of her exhibitions. Today she is considered one of Germany's most significant painters. Aside from the world-famous (self) portraits there are also a number of lanscapes in the collection.

The **Roselius Haus** (3), next door to the Kunstschau, was the first house that Roselius bought. The original packing house was transformed in 1928 by Eduard Eeg into a representative city house that now serves as a museum of cultural history. The somewhat chaotic and materialistic collection (Roselius wanted to present an »ideal picture of a historic, north-German household« and not an art collection) displays valuable works from the 12th to 19th centuries. Almost unnnoticed by the general public, works by such greats as Tilman Riemenschneider, Lucas Cranach, Ludger tom Ring can be found here, as well as the silver treasure trove of the »Blackheads of Riga«.

Museums in Böttcher Street
Paula Modersohn-Becker Museum
Ludwig Roselius Museum
Collection Bernhard Hoetger
Tue–Sun 11am–6pm, Tel. 3388222.
www.museen-boettcherstrasse.de

On the small square in front of the Roselius House you will have a good view of the **House of Glockenspiel** (4). Several times a day, the 30 Meissen porcelain bells ring out from their decorative framework. January-March at 12pm, 3pm, 6pm, and April-December every hour from 12-6pm. The Glockenspiel was created by the musician Lutz Dietze, who had been a specialist for such bells

The Meissener porcelain bells of the Glockenspiel in Böttcherstraße make special music

at the Meißen works. In 1933, however, Dietze, a Jehovah's Witness, was arrested for his religious beliefs and imprisoned in the concentration camp Burg Hohnstein. His former employers at the Meißen company got him released and brought to Bremen especially for this project. However, after its completion in May, 1934, Dietze was imprisoned again, and died in 1936 as a result of his ordeal. The glockenspiel plays ten different songs to accompany a cycle of colorful plaques representing »ocean conquerors« through the ages. The rugged carved faces of Leif Erikson, Christopher Columbus, Charles Lindbergh and others are revealed when a hidden window in one of the corner towers opens especially for the Glo-

1 Paula Becker-Modersohn Haus
2 Handwerkerhof
3 Roselius House
4 House of Glockenspiel
5 Hoetgerhof
6 House St. Petrus
7 House Atlantis
8 Robinson-Crusoe-House

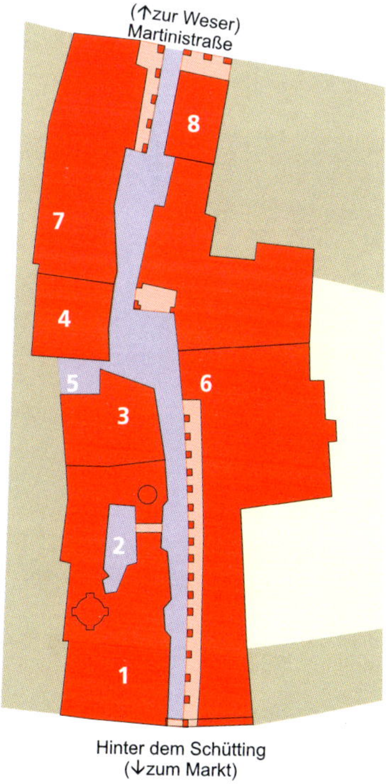

ckenspiel. In the **Hoetgerhof** (5), you will experience an entirely different atmosphere. This quiet corner is the perfect place to take a minute to contemplate the various works of Hoetger displayed there.

The **House St. Petrus** (6), built 1923–1927 now accommodates the »Ständige Vertretung« a restaurant with historical photos of the earlier Federal Republic of Germany.

House Atlantis (7), at the end of Böttcherstraße, is an impressive modern building, though its exterior today is very different from the original, of which only a few features remain. Hoetger's steel, glass and cement foyer and stairwell was one of the most beautiful expressionist spaces of his time. The stairway leads to the "Himmelsaal" (Sky Room). The chapel-like room's ceiling is composed of blue glass elements. The original facade of the house depicted a huge figure that resembled both Odin and Jesus Christ figure. This was completely decimated by the one Allied bomb that fell in Böttcherstraße. The facade you see today was created by Ewald Mataré.

Roselius-bust by Bernhard Hoetger, 1922

In 1931, Karl von Weihe constructed the **Robinson-Crusoe-House** (8) across the way from the House Atlantis, and thus reminded of the popular novel character, whose father was from Bremen (in the novel). It contains a café on the ground floor and a gallery specialized in craft exhibitions.

Many visitors from abroad couldn't even guess at the street's history during the Nazi period. Roselius, a sympathizer of the Nazi party, viewed Böttcher Street as a display of nationalist faith and hoped for support from the party leadership. Hitler himself, however, condemned the street as »degenerate art« and only Roselius' influence kept it from being torn down.

After stepping out of narrow, sheltered Böttcherstraße, you will find yourself on the busy four-lane thoroughfare of Martinistraße, a very effective barrier between the city and the river. Many wish this ugly, difficult-to-cross street gone. All except wheelchair-users can go through the subterranean passage just a few steps to the right of the Böttcherstraße exit, which will lead you directly to the Weser.

Wheelchair-users, however, will need to go to the surface pedestrian crossing with traffic light approximately 40 meters away.

Ships on the »Schlachte« promenade

Weser Promenade and Schlachte

Upon emerging from the pedestrian tunnel, you will find yourself on the Martini Quay. From here, you can take a **boat tour** of the Neustadt Harbor, the only inner-city harbor which, along with the »Industriehafen,« still has significant freight traffic. Yet it is worth the 90-minute boatride along the Schlachte into the harbor areas, if only for the impressive panoramas or river and shore.

Other cruises that depart from the **Martini Quay** include those down to Bremerhaven or up the river to the Weserwehr. From the harbor cruise, at your request to the ship's personnel upon boarding, you can disembark at the Pier 2 cultural event center in Gröpelingen, in the western part of the city. (Please inform the staff at the beginning of your journey that you want to get off at PIER 2.)

New in the cruise programme is the tour through the 100-year-old **Industriehafen**, formerly closed to the public, in the western part of the city. This includes six harbour bays, accommodating 2,000 foreign ships per year, around 3,000 employees, with a turnover of six million tons of goods per year. The Industriehafen has numerous private freight and production facilities. It is an important part of the Bremen Harbour economy. Around half of the freight turn-over of Bremen happens here. Steel, coal, coke, construction materials, marble and other natural stone, fishmeal, junk metal and mineral oils all come through this harbor. The tour (circa 2.5 hours) takes place only once per month. (Details at www.hal-oever.de)

Harbor Tours

Hal Över Shipping Company, An der Schlachte 2, Tel. 338989, Open Mon–Fri. 9am–5pm, Nov.-March 9am–3pm

If a cruise is not in your plans, however, you can also enjoy the maritime atmosphere from solid land, on the Schlachte. Though the Weser can only accommodate small ships and sport yachts at this point on the river, from the **Schlachte**

(C) you can still enjoy a fresh salty breeze, the circling seagulls, and you feel close to the sea. After the extensive development of the Schlachte to the city's maritime promenade, many ships have dropped anchor, most of which can be visited. Of particular historical interest is the 14th century replica of a Hanseatic **»Kogge«,** the merchant ship that served an area from Scandinavia to Southern France, bringing Bremen her initial wealth. In January 2014, a defective seacock caused the »Kogge« to sink at its dock. It, however, was raised already the next day, and now will be put to rights again.

Less spectacular but just as important is the nearly 30-meter, 1½-mast **Weserbarge »Franzius«**. This is a replica of the kind of boat that was the most important means of transport for Bremen and the surrounding area into the 19th Century. The replica of the **40-gun frigate »Admiral Nelson«** is especially fun for the children: not only is it exactly like the pirate ship you always imagined, the restaurant on board specializes in pancakes of every possible flavor and kind, making a visit a must.

In 2016 the tall ship **»Alexander von Humboldt«** was relocated to the Schlachte. The ship received world wide popularity in 1988 when it appeared with green sails in numerous commercials for the Bremen brewery Becks. The ship, built in 1906 and named after the German natural scientist, will be home to a restaurant and a hotel business in the future.

The name **»Schlachte«** has a remarkable etymology. Historically, it can be traced to the Low German verb »slait« which translates as »to embed or pound in«, recalling the original building of the harbor. The early Bremen merchants had bought a stretch of sandy riverside and arranged for heavy wooden planks to be driven into the sand to provide a solid anchorage for their ships. Over the centuries, the stone wall and wide quay were built to serve the ever-increasing traffic. Here, goods were unloaded and inspected. Afterwards, the tobacco, sugar, fish, spice, coffee

The harbor tours start at Martini-Pier

Beer garden on the »Schlachte« promenade

and much more would be packed and stored in the warehouses on the high ground of the Schlachte.

This was sailors' own part of the city – with counting houses, inns, bathhouses, pubs, and bordellos – separated from the rest of Bremen by a wall. Only a street name »Schlachtpforte« or »Schlachte Gate« and the church **St. Martini** (B) recall the pulsing life of this former harbor area. When the Weser silted in and ships could no longer reach the city, the Schlachte lost its importance.

St. Martini, above the Martini Quay, was built in 1230 for the seafaring families who sought God's blessing before the ships went to sea. The steep brick walls were built in 1371 to protect the church from the flood waters of the Weser, a continual hazard. Four times per day (9:15. 12:15, 15:15, 18:15), the bells in the massive tower ring the well-known hymn »Lobe den Herrn« (Praise the Lord). These chimes also honor the Pietist minister of the church, **Joachim Neander** (1650–1680), who lived in the attached vicarage on the western side of the church. These rooms are now named for him, »Neanderhaus«. Evening on the Schlachte is even better than daytime. You will enjoy the many first quality international restaurants and well-populated beer gardens with their good view of the water and unique atmosphere.

Information on events, restaurants, and boat trips
www.schlachte.de

The **Theaterschiff** (theater ship), offering a variety of evening entertainment, such as cabaret and comedy, is moored on Quai 4.

Theaterschiff Bremen e.V.
Tiefer 104, Tel. 7908600,
www.theaterschiff-bremen.de

The striking architecture of the youth hostel

A stroll downriver along the Schlachte is especially worthwhile, The walk will take you past a variety of ships offering dining and entertainment, all part of Bremen's new media district. While the path down along the Weser offers a view of the happenings riverside, the promenade above allows glimpses into this interesting new quarter. Originally the **Stephanivorstadt**, or Steven's District, was located here, which in the middle ages belonged to the craftsmen, whose simple houses pressed close together around the gothic St. Stephani Church. The entire district and the historic packing houses on the riverbanks were destroyed in the course of the war.

Only recently did the area receive renewed attention and fundmental improvements.

In the immediate area is the **Designer Hotel Überfluss**, whose ambitiously constructed foyer is a must. Lamps by Tom Dixon and chairs designed by Charles Eames are just a few of the finer points of the interior decoration, which was carried out by the Dutch design team »Concrete« of Amsterdam. The architects Kastens and Sieman utilized fragments of historical buildings for the construction of the building, which can be found on the hotel's façade and elsewhere.

A few steps further you will wee the unmistakable green-and-yellow cube of the recently renovated and expanded **Youth Hostel** (D). If you should see the young people enjoying the evening on the large terrace, you might just be tempted to trade your hotel room for a bunk bed, the location is so beautiful.

At the center of the new district are **Radio Bremen**'s new offices (E), where it has been ever since moving from the city's outskirts in 2007. The

Radio Bremen's new home in the »Faulen Quartier«

architectural challenge of this building lay in respecting the aesthetic of the medieval streets while constructing the new radio center. Architect Jürgen Böge drafted three buildings, the interiors of which contain state-of-the-art broadcasting facilities and technology, while the exteriors fit into the local architecture. The Weserhaus on the Schlachte houses further offices of Germany's Public Media Agency ARD. The three-meter tall »Caller« was placed in front of the building, a sculpture produced for Radio Bremen Television by **Gerhard Marcks** in 1967.
The Diepenau building in the middle, serves as the main entrance to the smallest ARD center, which contains the organization's most modern studios.
Just behind the third building lies the **Bamberger Haus** (F), the headquarters of the public educational institution, Volkhochschule Bremen (VHS). The building, rich in tradition, stood empty for an extended period and wasn't renovated until 2007. Constructed in 1929 by the Jewish businessman Julius Bamberger the department store enjoyed considerable popularity in its time, especially among the working class. After several years of defamation and persecution under the Nazis, Bamberger gave up and fled to the United States, where he died in 1951. The restoration of this historical building is a monument in honor of this persecuted citizen. On the ground floor, a small exhibition on the life of Julius Bamberger can be found.
The path leads back to the district, past the church **St. Stephani** (G), which was badly damaged in the war. The ou-

The Legend of the Seven Lazy Brothers

The Bremen literary figure Friedrich Wagenfeld (1810–1846) created the story of the Seven Lazy Brothers, on which Berhnard Hoetger's fountain in the »Handwerkerhof« (Craftsman Courtyard) is based.
The story goes as follows: a farmer once owned extensive land, which unfortunately had such poor soil that it produced very little. In some places, it was so sandy and dry that the cabbage simply wilted and died. In other places, it was so swampy that the hay growing there would barely suffice for their one cow. This farmer had seven sons who were so lazy that they didn't mind watching their father work himself to death, rather than help him. One day, the seven brothers went out into the world. After many years, they returned, and to the astonishment of the neighbors and their own father, they built good roads and dug wells, as they had seen people do in neighboring Holland. The neighbors, however, saw these innovations with great suspicion and only gossiped, »Those boys are as lazy as ever! They're too lazy to want to work on wet fields or clean their muddy shoes – and rather than walk all the way to the Weser for water, they have gone and dug wells!

This picture shows how it looked like in the area arround St. Stephani after the war

ter walls are an excellent example of the Gothic brickwork of the 13th and 14th centuries. Under National Socialism the congregation was a center of Church-based resistance to the regime. Today it serves as a center for cultural events. The path now leads back to the Weser, where the B75 and the railway line to Oldenburg cross the river. These are the last bridges over the river – further toward the North Sea, the Weser can only be crossed by ferry (or via the Weser tunnel south of Bremerhaven).
Behind the railway bridge, a high fence blocked the passage until a few years ago: Here began the **Freihafen** (free port), the vast area of the city's ports of Bremen. Today, the new promenade leads to one of the most exciting new urban areas of Bremen, the Überseestadt (see bicycle tour page 69).
Back on the Weser, past the B-75, the pedestrian bridge offers access to the other side of the river. The walkway along the dike leads to the famed **Beck's Brewery & Co.** (H). The old Bremen company has been purchased by an international corporation, but tours through the brewery are still possible.

Exclusive brewery tour
Several times daily: Guided brewery tours, bookable via Bremer Touristik-Zentrale (BIZ) (Duration approx. 3 hrs), Tel. 3080010

Further on, in the direction of the city center, you will soon find the Teerhof (Tar Yard Island), a natural island in the middle of the river. A few hundred meters further lies the **Künstler-House** (I), which offers excellent cuisine.
The 16 studios are made available for various artistic disciplines (including painting, film, photography, installation, sculpture, performance), and assigned by an expert jury.

Künstlerhaus
Wed–Sun 2–7pm
www.kuenstlerhausbremen.de

Restaurant Am Deich 68
Tue –Sun, open from 18:00 on,
Tel. 5979682

Around this point you can cross a pedestrian bridge to the Teerhof (Tar Yard), now filled with modern apartment buildings.

Notice the American conceptual artist Lawrence Weiner's playful inscription on the outer walls of the former Coffee-Roastery: HAVING BEEN BUILT ON SAND WITH ANOTHER BASE (BASIS) IN FACT. AUF SAND GEBAUT TATSÄCHLICH AUF (AUS) ANDEREM GRUND.

The **Teerhof** (Tar Yard) (K) was in fact nothing more than a sand dune in the river. In the Middle Ages the city dockyards were located here and it was here that the ships were tarred as part of their waterproofing, a task that brought with it fire hazards and had to be situated a safe distance away from the city. In the 19th century an entire district of warehouses, of a characteristic steep, thin form, were placed here. These were completely destroyed in the Second World War, however, and it took several decades before an urban development contest was held to kick off new construction there. At the beginning of the 1990s, an exclusive residential quarter was constructed, the buildings of which suggest the style of the earlier warehouses.

The white lettern refer to two excellent institutions for contemporary art: the

Visiting the world's famous brewery »Becks« at their Museum

View of the Weserburg Museum für moderne Kunst

Weserburg Museum of modern art (J) presents international works of art from the last 40 years on over 6000 square meters. The Weserburg is not only Germany's first museum collection, it is also its largest museum for present-day art. Edward Kienholz, George Segal, Richard Serra, Andy Warhol, Morris Louis, Donald Judd, Sol LeWitt, Mario Merz, Richard Long, Georg Baselitz and Gerhard Richter, among others, are or were at one time in these rooms. The collections rotate, and there are frequent special exhibitions.

Weserburg Museum für moderne Kunst Museum of Modern Art)
Teerhof Teerhof 20, Tel. 598390,
Tue–Sun 11am–6pm,
www.weserburg.de

In the same building you can also find the **Gesellschaft für Aktuelle Kunst** (Society for Contemporary Art). Since 1980, this art association has dedicated itself to representing current artistic trends through exhibitions and projects. Its aim is to engage us on controversial subjects in both art and society in the city.
Aside from large exhibitions, the Society for Contemporary Art offers glimpses into the present-day art scene through films, electronic music and public art in and around Bremen.

Gesellschaft für Aktuelle Kunst
Teerhof 21, Tel. 500897, Tue-Sun 11am-6pm, www.gak-bremen.de

Going across another elegant pedestrian bridge (with elevators), you can return to the Schlachte, where the setting sun and the beer-gardens invite you to take a break.

right: Evening sun at the Weser

AKB
SCHNOO
OASE
Die Adresse für

Tour 3
Bremen's Oldest Quarter – The Schnoor

Like pearls on a string, the small, picturesque houses that line the streets here give this quarter its name, **»Schnoor,«** translated »string«. Thousands of visitors per year seek out these pretty, peaceful streets to stroll or shop, watch the craftsmen at work in their shops, or enjoy one of the many cafés or restaurants. The Schnoor is truly an oasis in the bustle of the city. If you want fast food or retail chains, you won't find them here: originality and artistry are watchwords amongst the shop and restaurant proprietors in the Schnoor. But even after closing time, this quarter is lively with cultural activities. Just two of these, are the **Teatro Magico** and the **Rosenak-Haus**, a small museum of the Jewish community in Bremen.
On your way through the Schnoor, you are likely to run into a very strange figure: On the »Wüstestätte« limping and hunchbacked, his wooden leg out to trip you, is **»Heini Holtenbeen«** (Pegleg Heini). Crippled after a severe accident, he lived in poverty in the house at Im Schnoor #8. Working occasionally and begging, he made a meager living. Meanwhile, however, he became known throughout the city for his sharp tongue, spouting sayings and remarks in Low German dialect. He died in 1908 in the St. Jürgen Asylum. From a photograph, this lifesize bronze statue of him was created to memorialize this remarkable character representative of Schnoor residents of a former age, for, in the 19th Century, only the poorest of the poor lived in this part of the city.

Yet in earlier times, the Schnoor had been the vital seed of the city's growing economy. From the 13th century on, craftsmen, fishermen, and seafarers populated this area, building their little reed-covered huts on what was then an island between the wild Weser and its subsidiary arm, the Balge (no longer there). This risky area down at the base of the safe dune where the church had been built, attracted people who sought the prosperity that the river could give them. These people were the foundation for Bremen's later wealth. This was the location of the

The statue of Heini Holtenbeen, a 19th Century Bremen character

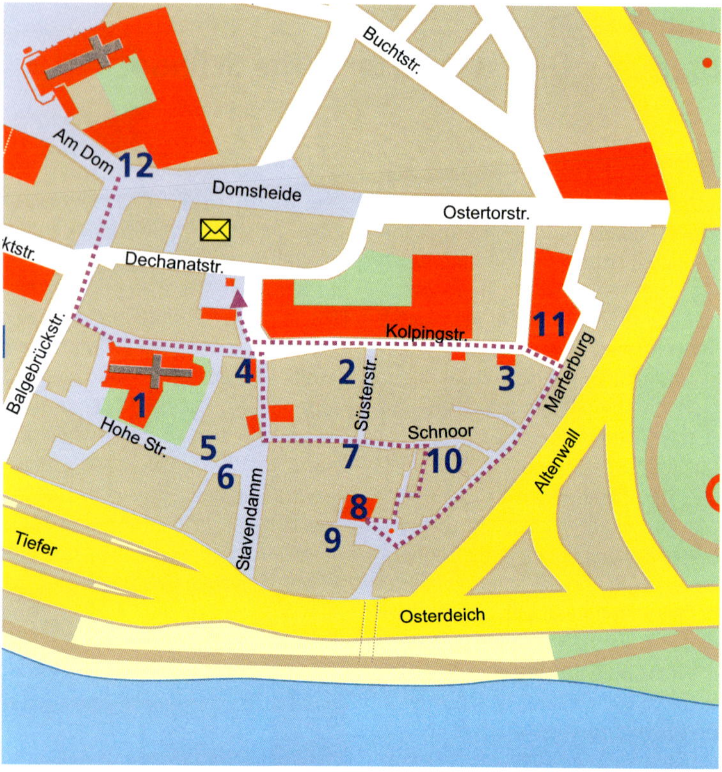

1	**St. Johann**
2	**Birgitten-Kloster**
3	**Former synagogue**
4	**Gasthof »Kaiser Friedrich«**
5	**Schifferhaus**
6	**Fountain**
7	**Hochzeitshaus**
8	**Packhaus, Bremer Geschichtenhaus**
9	**Sculpture Heini Holtenbeen**
10	**Institute for Plattdeutsch**
11	**post-modern residential area**
12	**Meeting point: Tour with the Night Watchman**

first ferry over the river, and later, of the first bridge. Around 1244, Franciscan Monks built a monastery here, and later, in the 14th century, the Church **St. Johann** (1), with its massive, confident brick facade. During the Reformation, the Franciscans were driven out and the church was used as a hospital. In

The ornamental brick of
St. Johann Catholic church

1816, however, it was returned to the use of Bremen's Catholic minority. In 1871/72, the Gothic interior was reconstructed on the simple, clean lines that you see today.

In 2002, for the first time since the Reformation, a Catholic monastery was established in Bremen. Not far from the former monastery of the Franciscans, the Sisters of Birgit gave Bremen architect Ulrich Tilgner the contract to design their bright and colorful postmodern **monastery** (2), Birgitten-Kloster. The sisters welcome all, from the merely stressed to the hard-pressed, to »find spirit and peace of mind« as they take part in the quiet and meditative life of the cloister.

In the 19th century, the Schnoor was a place for those on the edge of society – the poor and the different, namely Catholics and Jews who, until the Revolution of 1918, did not even enjoy the full rights of citizens. It is not surprising, thus, that the Schnoor was also the site of the **synagogue** (3) from 1876 onwards, No. 6 on what is now Kolpingstraße. During the notorious »Reich's Pogrom Night« during the night of November 9/10, 1938, the synagogue was torched by the SA, along with the members of the fire department and other citizens.

From Kolpingstraße, you will pass by the **Gasthof »Kaiser Friedrich«** (4) directly into the center of the Schnoor. Of the medieval settlement, nothing remains. The oldest houses are from the 15th century, and every succeeding era has made its own architectural contributions. During the Second World War, not a single bomb fell into this area, yet, because the people's poverty made renovation or even repair unfeasible, by the mid-1950s, the quarter was a shambles. In 1959, very much counter to the zeitgeist of the '50s – to demolish and make way for »modern« buildings – the

Striking new building:
the Birgitten Cloister

Senate decided to undertake a thorough restoration of the area. After tireless persuasion on the part of **Karl Dillschneider**, then in charge of caring for city monuments and historic buildings, instead of erecting a »modern shopping and business area« as planned, the city approved the Schnoor restoration project. With subsidies from the city, the inhabitants were encouraged to work in close contact with city historians and architects to repair and restore their houses. The interiors of these houses were often completely modernized, while the facades were retained or reconstructed in stylistically appropriate ways. The Schnoor became the collecting place for countless sculptured stones, roof ornaments, coats of arms, vases, friezes, columns and other decorative elements rescued from the rubble all over Bremen and integrated into the »new« Schnoor. Thus the Schnoor displays many an architectural souvenir of Bremen as it was before the war.

Artists and craftsmen also discovered the special atmosphere of the place and bought houses, apartments and ateliers there. This is what makes every shop window – where you can still observe many of the craftsmen at their work – a new discovery.

The small **Schifferhaus** (5) in Stavendamm was once a general store where the seafarers who moored on the We-

The old Schifferhaus in Schnoor

ser bought supplies. Wolfgang Loose bought and renovated the house, and it is him who is to thank for the extensive Schnoor Archive containing countless photos of the quarter before and directly after the war. Since 2007, the archive is located in the "Bremer Geschichtenhaus" (House of History). Interested parties can contact the Schnoor Archive by phone at 3362651 (appointments are required for visits).
Around the 15th century, this area was known for its bath houses, which served sailors after their long voyages. The **fountain** (6) by Jürgen Cominotto depicts a typical scene in the bath house – at least as the artist imagined it.
The **Bremen Press Club** is located in the Waldemar Koch Haus on Straße Im Schnoor. The club was founded in 1971 by Bremen journalists, and is a forum for public debates and discussions. Along with their restaurant and meeting rooms, the Bremen Press Club regularly presents photo exhibits.
From the Schnoor, a tiny street leads to the Wüstestätte. At the narrowest

The Schnoor is especially charming during Advent

The Schnoor Quarter lies in the shadow of the cathedral

»Jacobus Major« figure in the façade of the old Packhaus

point of this street is the **Hochzeitshaus** (7), or »Wedding House.« Probably the smallest hotel in the world, it consists of only one room. In the Middle Ages, couples would come from the country to the city to marry in the cathedral and would spend the night in such »wedding houses«. The Hochzeitshaus is a modern variation of the historic establishment – special, but not only for honeymoons.

The long outsider tradition of the Schnoor has yet another wonderful witness: **Jacobus Major** over the entry to the **Packhaus** (8). Jacobus the Elder, one of Christ's followers, was executed by Herod after returning from an unsuccessful missionary trip in Spain. According to the saint's legend, his body was transported miraculously across the Mediterranean back to Santiago de Compostela, which was to become one of the most popular places of pilgrimage in Christendom. Jacobus, with his symbol of the seashell, became the patron saint of pilgrims and travelers. His likeness was displayed to show pilgrims the way to **Jacobus inns** where they would be welcome.

The Jacobi Majores Brothers, founded in 1656, carried on this medieval

In the History House, Bremen's past comes alive

View of the post-modern Marterburg

tradition of hospitality and bought a house on the Wüstestätte which would shelter poor widows.

Today the **Bremer Geschichtenhaus**, Bremen History House, is located in the former Packing House. Various figures tell visitors stories from the history of the city, stretching from the 17th to the 20th centuries. The famed Heini Holtenbeen, the poisoner Gesche Gottfried, the Bremer Fisch Lucie – all are brought to life to joy of children.

Bremer Geschichtenhaus
Stavendamm 8, Tel. 3362651, Mon 12–18:00, Tue–Sun 11–18:00, www.bremer-geschichtenhaus.de

At the heart of the Schnoor lies the **Institute for Plattdeutsch** (10), or »Low German.« Equipped with an extensive library, they have taken on the task of maintaining and spreading the traditional dialect, literature and culture of this area with their regular readings and presentations.

Across the street is the **Künstlerhaus Ausspann**, a broadly inclusive culture and gastronomy project with special offers for refugees living in Bremen, among others. Superb coffee and excellent cuisine awaits every guest.

Ausspann Künstlerhaus
Schnoor 1-2 , Tel. 0176-83105402, Tue - Thu 3pm–10pm, Fri–Sun 11am–10pm, www.ausspann-bremen.de

In the 1980s, architects Goldapp and Klump realized a bright **post-modern residential area** (11) on the Marterburg at the eastern exit of the Schnoor. This area playfully uses the architectural language of the Schnoor and the monumental buildings just above it.

Tour 4
Through the Wallanlagen (Battlement Park)

In 1802, when the old defensive installations at Bremen's city wall were to be dismantled, it was lucky for the city that the land was not simply given up for building. Instead, the Senate founded a »Committee to Plan and maintain Public Walks,« with the task of turning the Wallanlangen or »Battlements« into flower gardens, verdant nooks and lawns. Court gardener **Christian Ludwig Bosse** (1771 – 1832) proposed a remarkable plan for the former military grounds: to create »a sunny English garden offering views such as nature does in her most beautiful regions.« By means of clever use of the existing ridges and valleys, plateaus, soft cliffs, perspectives, and water, and by smart laying of paths and planting, they achieved the excitement of wilderness combined with the aesthetic qualities of an artwork.

In 2002, the Bicentennial celebration of the park's creation provided the occasion to reconstitute it in original form. It is especially charming to start your exploration of the Wall Park at the Schlachte. From the **»Martini Quay«** to between the Stephani Bridge and a railway bridge, the promenade widens to a sort of broad, square terrace, on which you will find an old brick wall with a wrought iron gate marking the **entrance to the Park** (1). At the end of the 17th century, this was the location of the poorhouse, which was later used as the first Focke Museum, Bremen's museum of local history and culture. Ever since World War II when the baroque building was destroyed, the surrounding gardens at the western tip of the city center have lain dreamily abandoned. A tangle of busy streets built in the frenzy to modernize after the war now cut through the park. Pedestrians can make their way over footbridges and through tunnels to reach the steep **Sand Dune Bastion** (2), one of seven former bastions, all of which had windmills on them. On the other side of the Bürgermeister-Smidt-Straße you will see an **old toll house** in which the City Parks Commission now provides information on the Wallanlagen (Battlement Park).

Your way will lead you back past old oaks, elms and lime trees to the **Gießhaus Bastion** on which the single remaining **windmill** (3) now stands. In 1998, the windmill was extensively restored, and the interiors were converted into a modern restaurant. Enjoy excellent coffee and cake with a view of the old ramparts. the windmill is a good place for a rest.

On the Herdentorsteinweg, you will see the **Steinhäuser-Vase** (4), a Carrara marble decoration from 1856, in the shade of a 200-year-old hazelnut tree originally from Asia Minor.

A few steps further along, all paths come together at the **Bischofsnadel** (5), or »Bishop's Needle«, a narrow tunnel through the wall into the city. In former times, this entrance leading directly to the cathedral and the city

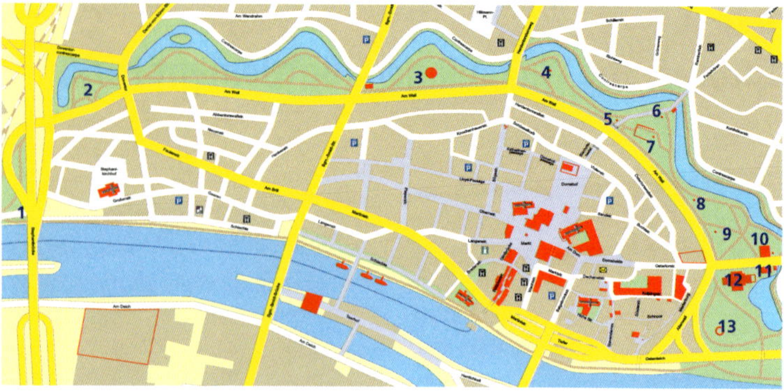

1 **Entrance Focke-Garten**
2 **Sand Dune Bastion**
3 **Windmill**
4 **Steinhäuser-Vase**
5 **Bischofsnadel**
6 **Rosselenker**
7 **Theater Garden**
8 **Lidice memorial**
9 **Monument for Olbers**
10 **Wilhelm Wagenfeld Haus**
11 **Gerhard-Marcks-Haus**
12 **Kunsthalle**
13 **Altmannshöhe**

hall was the only one that the bishop and his servants were allowed to use. Near the mouth of the tunnel is a Bernd Altenburg frieze of a running man whose upper body merges into a wall. Later, someone added a pithy, (now well-loved) graffito: »With glasses, this wouldn't have happened…«

The path along the water is usually very busy and well-populated: it is a principal junction for bike riders heading towards the train station, Schwachhausen, and the University. While natives hurry by, however, the visitor should pause a moment to enjoy the **Rosselenker** (6), »The Boy leading a Stallion«, a bronze by Louis Tuaillon (1900). In Calvinistic Bremen of the time, the naked boy was the subject of turbulent criticism.

The path along the water soon takes a steep upward turn to the **Theater Garden** (7). On top of the Theaterburg was Bremen's first theater, built in 1843. This, however, was destroyed during World War II. In 1965, the ruins finally made way for gardens. On this quiet site of the former theater you will find Gerhard Marcks' Die Liegende, »The Prone,« posing daily for students of the art school. At the foot of the Theaterberg is a **memorial** (8) for the inhabitants of the Bohemian village, Lidice, whose citizens were slaughtered on June 10, 1942 by the Waffen SS reacting to the assassination of Reinhard Heydrich. The Lidice memorial, reminiscent of the charred remnants of the village, was created by Jürgen Waller as a counterpoint to the 1936 statue, "Sterbender Jüngling" (Dying Boy). The 1936 piece recalled right-wing soldiers killed in the suppression of the "Bremer Räterepublik," an independent socialist communist government constituted of radical workers' and soldiers' councils, that took over Bremen for a 3-month

The Lidice Memorial in Battlement Park (Wallanlagen)

period in 1918-19. On yet another hill, you will find a statue (9) in honor of the doctor and hobby astronomer **Wilhelm Olbers** (1758–1840), who is known among astronomers as the discoverer of the planetoids Pallas, Ceres, and Vesta. From this hill, go down the gentle slope to three of Bremen's most important museums.

The **Wilhelm Wagenfeld Haus** (10) on the street Am Wall is dedicated to showing the work of the internationally well-known Bremen industrial designer of that same name. Up until just a few years ago, this former guard-house at the city border was used as a temporary prison for illegal aliens awaiting deportation. One room in the museum recalls this darker side of its history. The 19th century guardhouse on the opposite side of the street is now the **Gerhard-Marcks-Haus** (11). Since 1971, the building has been a museum of contemporary sculpture, primarily exhibiting the work of Marcks. 300 sculptures and 12,000 prints comprise the practically inexhaustible fund that allows the works to be arranged and re-arranged in ever-new thematic perspectives. Also, contemporary sculptors are regularly invited to show their work in this popular space. With unorthodox exhibition concepts and collaborative projects, the sculpture museum succeeds well in attracting a younger clientel.

Das ehemalige Akzisehäuschen beherbergt heute das Gerhard-Marcks-Haus

In 1847, the **Kunsthalle** (12) was built according to the plans of Lüder Rutenberg, becoming an art museum of international standing, now privately run by the »Kunstverein in Bremen«.

In the Gerhard-Marcks House, the most important sculpture museum of Northern Germany

The Bremen Kunsthalle

The Kunsthalle displays European paintings from the 14th century to the present, focusing on French and German art of the 19th and 20th centuries, including works by Manet, Monet, Liebermann, Slevogt and Corinth. Over 200,000 copperplate engravings, the museum's Kupferstichkabinett, formed the collection's origin and remain one of the largest copperplate collections in Europe.

The history of the Kunsthalle is closely linked to the name of its first director, Gustav Pauli, who fearlessly acquired the works of avant-garde artists of his time like Corot, French Impressionists and the then controversial »The Poppy Field« by Van Gogh. Today, the Kunsthalle remains open to innovative contemporary art and its exhibits currently include works by John Cage, Olafur Eliasson and James Turrell, whose three-story work »Above - Between - Below« is integrated into the museum building. With an expansion that opened in 2011, symmetry was restored to the old building in the form of two new cubic side wings. The resulting architecture combines the historical fabric with new elements in a contrasting and harmonious way. Since then, the Kunsthalle has featured state-of-the-art technology and significantly more space - for the museum café **Sylvette**, as well as for the museum's educational programs, which are central to its mission.

Those who wish to take a longer break can do so at the restaurant **Canova**, facing a quiet lake adjacent to the Kunsthalle (Tue-Sat 10am-10pm, Sun 10am-7pm). The restaurant was named after the Italian sculptor, **Antonio Canova** (1757 – 1822) whose classicistic marble work »Psyche« is in the possession of the Kunsthalle.

Wilhelm Wagenfeld Haus

Am Wall 209, Tel. 3399933, Tue. 3pm – 9pm, Wed – Sun 10am – 6pm, Tours Sun at 1pm and by appointment, www.wilhelm-wagenfeld-stiftung.de

Gerhard-Marcks-Haus

Am Wall 208, Tel. 327200, Tue – Sun 10am – 6pm, Thu. 10am – 9pm, www.marcks.de

Gerhard Marcks: Die Liegende (The Prone). Statue in the Wallanlangen

Kunsthalle Bremen
Am Wall 207, Tel. 329080,
Tue. 10am – 9pm, Wed – Sun
10am – 5pm,
www.kunsthalle-bremen.de

Behind the Kunsthalle, still in the Wallanlagen (Battlement Park), the path ascends one last time to **Altmannshöhe** (13), »Altmann's Hill,« a memorial dedicated to the fallen German soldiers of World War I, as well as the more controversial dead of the Free Corps Gerstenberg and Caspari, counter-revolutionary paramilitary groups, and three Nazi Party members, stylized at the time as »pure blood witnesses«. (These three last and most controversial were removed after the war.) The Nazis used the

Bremen is young

Walk around in the »Viertel« of Ostertor – or observe your companions drinking beer on the »Schlachte;« you will find you are surounded by young people. Nearly 20,000 students attend the University of Bremen; 10,000 more are studying at the Technical School (»Hochschule«). But Bremen is also the place of choice for apprenticeships or other training – in logistics, renewable energy, or for air, space, and automobile technology – attracting the young and energetic from all over Germany. Young families, too, come for the compact neighborhoods and good social and cultural infrastructure of Bremen. Add to these, the large families descending from the migrants of the 1960s, and in some parts of the city, you have a trend that defies the demographics at work in the rest of baby-boomer Germany.

Along with its many impressive artworks, Battlement Park is full of exotic trees and shrubs, brought home by Bremen's widely-travelled merchants

monument as a backdrop for proclamations and rallies.

The 1935 statue, **»The Mother,«** by Ernst Gorsemann, is also on Altmann's Hill. Taken down temporarily after the war, she was replaced after her typical war-time hairstyle was remodeled as a mourning veil. From this terrace, you will enjoy a great view of the Weser. Kerstin Doty, in her dedication essay for the Battlement Park's bicentennial, would write, »From this garden place, 200 years ago, the citizens of Bremen might observe the wild flow of the as yet unchanneled waters of the Weser«. On the other side of the river, you will also see the »Upside-down bureau dresser« of **Bremen's old waterworks**, built during the *Gründerzeit* (circa 1870s – 1900).

Tours in the »Wallanlagen« (Battlement Park)

StattReisen Bremen, Tel. 4305656,
www.stattreisen-bremen.de.
also BTZ

ROLAND MEHL

Tour 5
A new city is born – A bike tour through the Überseestadt

Approximately 2.5 hours, numerous restaurants and leisure spots.

In 1998, the people of Bremen watched with melancholy as the old **Überseehafen** – a harbor holding a century of tradition – was filled with Weser sand. This spectacle signaled the end of true harbor traffic in Bremen. Gone were the days when the entire family might stroll to the harbor on a Sunday afternoon to watch huge freighters and their crews from all over the world.
However, the harbor basins west of Bremen's city center had been unable to cope with ever-growing container ships for a long time. The once-booming port handling had almost completely relocated to Bremerhaven. Filling the first of three historic harbor basins was the beginning of a massive re-structuring of the 750-acre port area in the heart of the city.
This core area of Bremen where the new **Überseestadt** will be built by 2025 is 1 km wide and 3.5 km long. The state of Bremen intends to invest 350 million Euro by 2025 to provide the necessary infrastructure, with another two billion Euro are expected from private investors for construction of housing units.

Artists, ships, Weser-view

The bike tour through the Überseestadt is an excursion into the future of Bremen. At every turn, the ongoing construction efforts are creating new squares, public green spaces and above all, new architecture. The desired mix of trade, living and culture will – according to the planners – result in a new urbanity for a modern district.
By cycling along the river Weser, one can reach the Überseestadt from the St. Petri Cathedral in the heart of the city in about 10 minutes. Just a few years ago, it was not possible to access the port areas beyond the railway bridge. Today, a spacious and shining promenade leads straight to the striking **Weser Tower** (Am Weserterminal 1), the well-known star-architect Helmut Jahn's 22-story office building – the highest in Bremen – completed in 2010. This structure, elegantly lined with blue gleaming glass, is placed prominently right at the end of the Schlachte promenade.
In the shadow of the tower, two further buildings already house a variety of businesses: In 2013, the 4-star Steigenberger Hotel opened, lying directly on the water like an elegant ocean liner ready for departure. The hotel offers 139 rooms, as well as a large conference area and spa for hotel guests.
Many guests will spend an evening at the neighboring **Varieté-Theater** (1) operated by the GOP Entertainment Group. The GOP builds on the legendary Bremer Astoria of Emil Fritz, where stars such as Heinrich George, Theo Lingen, Lotte Werkmeister and Hans Moser performed between 1908 and its destruction in 1944. Today, however, the GOP is pursuing a new, contemporary concept, placing artis-

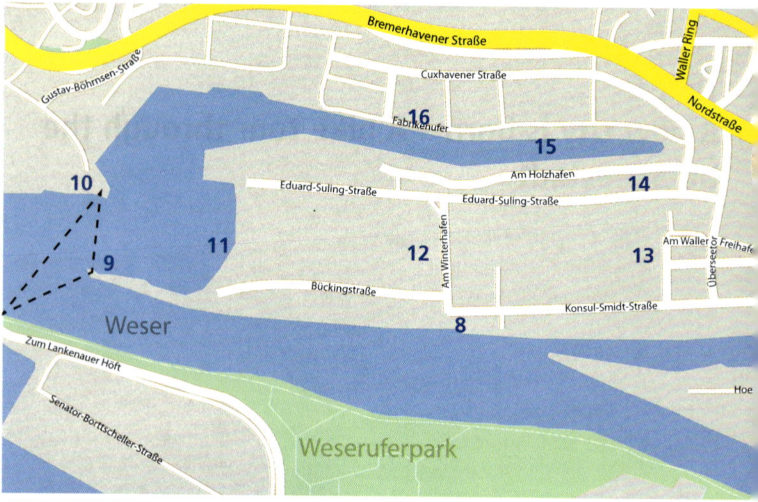

1	**GOP Varieté-Theater**
2	**Kaffee Quartier**
3	**Hilde-Adolf-Park**
4	**Kellogg's**
5	**Ehemaliger Europahafen**
6	**Marina Europahafen**
7	**Schuppen Eins**
8	**Landmark Tower**
9	**Molenturm**
10	**Pier 2 – Fährverbindung**
11	**Waller Sand**
12	**Überseepark**
13	**Großmarkt Bremen**
14	**Speicher XI**
15	**Holz- und Fabrikenhafen**
16	**Lloyd Caffee**

try and acrobatics at the center of the shows. Every two months, a new show program is revealed. At 400 seats, the GOP theater in Bremen is the largest of their six theaters nationwide. With excellent food, a piano bar (open every day from 6pm with live music, no show ticket required) and a dance club with Weser view, GOP promises unforgettable evenings of entertainment in Bremen.

GOP-Varieté
Am Weser Terminal 4,
Tel.: 89898989, www.variete.de

Further along the Weser river, we pass **WQ 1**, an office building resting on eye-catching slanted columns right on the water, designed by the internationally-known Hamburg architect Hadi Teherani. The all-glass façade guarantees maximal daylight in the offices with a magnificent view of the Weser. Opened in 2014, this remarkable building earned the approval of the Society for Sustainable Construction.

Through the coffee quarter to the overseas port

Our route now leads us away from the Weser, past the office buildings **Luv** and **Lee** (built in 2014 according to a design by Delugan Meissl Associated Architects, Vienna) into the former port area. Here, almost nothing now reminds one of the old harbor times. As a striking gateway to the new district - directly opposite the Jahn skyscraper – the seven-story office building **EINS**, by the Düsseldorf architecture firm StructureLab, was completed in 2016. The two slightly curved,

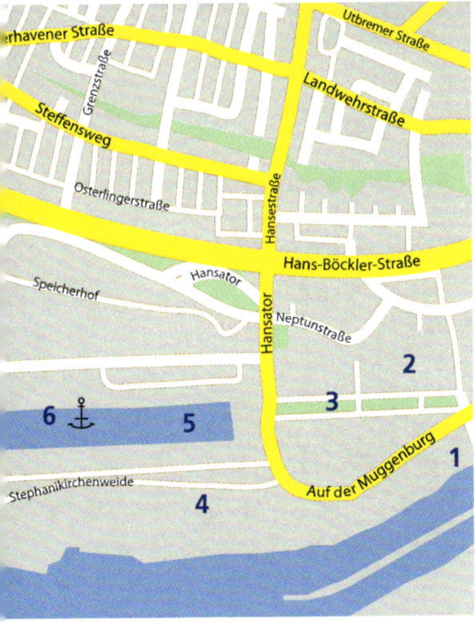

gleaming white buildings with an elegantly protruding flat roof offer 20,000 square meters of office space with flexible room concepts. On the ground floor, retail shops and restaurants have already emerged. Directly opposite, the **Kaffee Quartier** (2), a home for modern offices and convention rooms has presented itself in friendly and warm colors on the former site of a coffee roasting facility since 2017. The complex supplies employees with a cafeteria and a childcare center.
Next door is the first hostel in the Überseestadt, the **Zollhaus**. As the name suggests, the historical building occupies the old customs office at the former port entrance. This building saw the occasional discovery of contraband and witnessed the drama of smuggling arrests. It became legendary as a temporary dormitory for unaccompanied refugee youths from Syria until 2018. A band of Syrian and German musicians called the »Zollhaus Boys« was formed here. Today, they are an integral part of the Bremen music scene.
Next, we come to the **Hilde Adolf Park** (3), named to honor the well-known local politician of the SPD (Social Democratic Party of Germany), who died in 2002. The park lies amidst a wide, magnificent boulevard that leads westwards toward the Europahafen.
Numerous office buildings are being constructed along the park, notably the 13-story office building **Bömers Spitze**, with its distinctive tapered shape designed by the Bremen-based architects Hilmes Lamprecht. With the highest energy standard, green roof, solar technology and strikingly bright window fronts, this building offers over 11,000 square meters of office space and is one of the architectural landmarks of the Überseestadt.
Between the newly constructed office buildings, south of the park toward the Weser, there is striking evidence of another reality of the area: the older industrial establishments of the former port carry on with their operations. An eye-catching, soot-stained brick wall stands as witness to the 100 years of harbor tradition that formed the foundations of the neighborhood. Prominent amongst the traditional establishments is the bordering **Stroever Schellack Bremen**. The company recalls over 115 years on the

The historic Customs House (Zollhaust)

so-called **Muggenburg**, working with natural resins to manufacture a series of products including the old shellack records that predated vinyl records. In addition, these natural resins are also valuable basic ingredients in many pharmaceuticals, foods, and cosmetics products. Even more prominent amongst the older residents: **Kellogg's Bremen** (4). It began in 1962 with the Bremen Rice Merchants AG, which began to import Kellogg's products from the US company Kellogg's. Only shortly thereafter the Kellogg's Company founded its German subsidiary in Bremen. In 2017, the production of the popular breakfast cereals was discontinued. WPD, the wind park project developer, has now bought this area near the city center and is developing a new district, the »Überseeinsel«. Apartments right at the bank of the Weser, up to 1000 jobs and attractive architecture will be found here starting in 2021.

,The **Hilde-Adolf-Park** ends at the basin of the old **Europahafen** (5). Built in 1887, the harbor was considered one of the most modern installations in the world at that time. By the 1990s, the old piecemeal system of sheds, storerooms and railways connections had been lost to modern container traffic, the efficiency of which is undeniable. However, the old basin was too shallow and far from the open water for the gigantic new container ships. The Europahafen was finished. Nowadays the old harbor has become the center of the rapid new developments in the Überseestadt. Today, festivals, cultural and other events take place along the harbor basin. The two-day **Überseefestival**, a music festival organized by the non-profit association Musikszene Bremen e.V. Jazz, is particularly popular. During the breaks you can play table soccer under floodlights or simply relax by the harbor basin.

Info: www.musikszene-bremen.de

Along the Europahafen

There will be vigorous construction at the edge of the Europahafen for a few more years. Here, under the project name »Europahafenkopf«, an ensemble of four buildings designed by the four young Danish architects of the COBE office is being built. While office and living spaces are established on the upper floors, a market hall, retail and exhibition space, bicycle rental and car sharing will turn the ground floor area at the exposed harbor head into a public space.

We now cycle along the northern side of the Europahafen and pass the five port houses with exclusive living and office spaces. Among others, the **InnoLab** is located here, a cooperation of the Daimler Group with the agency Assassin Design. In the 350 square meter space, a think tank and research landscape has emerged with very few similarities to a conventional office, and bears more relation to the think tanks of companies such as Google, Twitter or Microsoft. »We have to get away from the desk if we want to be creative«, is the InnoLab's motto. The aim is to develop ideas for the work concepts of the future and to test new methods of cooperation: how will we communicate, how will we organize work, how canw e manage increasingly complex knowledge and develop the office of the future, which will then certainly not be called Office anymore. Next to these newly built port structures right on the northern edge of the basin, it is also worth having a look at the second row of buildings, such as **Speicher 1**, built in 1950 and converted into store-

New architecture in the old harbor: the LANDMARK TOWER

fronts and offices. The more than 200 m long and six-story tall building has been extensively and stylishly redesigned – the old planks partially reused – large, floor-to-ceiling windows and 4 meter high ceilings make the offices highly attractive. In September 2007, responding somewhat inadequately to the increasing need for parking, a 400-space structure opened next to the Speicher 1, the district garage – an interesting building with striking brown wood paneling. A new tram line will better connect the Überseestadt to the public transport in the future. Back at the harbor basin, the **marina** (6) opened in 2011. Sport boats up to 17 meters in length can anchor here, and passenger or ferry boats from 17 meters. There are even docking places for canoes, an interesting way to get onto the river, over the meadows and into the heart of the Überseestadt for an espresso.

Info: www.marina-europahafen.de

Meanwhile, at the edge of the harbor an interesting and varied **culinary scene** has emerged. For instance, Mohamed Subry bin Ahmed with his modern, authentic Asian cuisine, has won the hearts of those who are looking for a good meal during their lunch breaks. His JAYA is not only a gastronomic highlight, but also an important cooperation partner for the many initiatives, networks and events, organized by the companies, agencies and residents of the new district.

Responsible for the development of the Überseestadt is the Bremeninvest (WfB - Wirtschaftsförderung Bremen), which offers an up-to-date **culinary guide** of the Überseestadt to download. In it, you will find a good overview of the constantly changing and rapidly growing restaurant scene, including restaurants, cafés, bakeries, bistros and hip food trucks. We continue another three kilometers on the promenade directly along the harbor basin. Next stop: **Schuppen Eins** (7) (shed One) in the Konsul-Smidt-Straße 26. Such shallow sheds were once found along all the docks, and used to check and sort cargo for loading onto trucks or freight cars. You can get a good idea of

The marina at the basin of the Europahafen

the dimensions of the sheds in the restaurant **El Mundo** at the eastern part of the shed: The restaurant is located in one of the huge storage rooms. With massive chandeliers, tasteful decoration and a fantastic view of the harbor basin, the owners have succeeded in reinterpreting the historic architecture in a completely new way. Meanwhile, the entire Schuppen Eins is an exciting mix of companies, leisure activities, gastronomy and, among other things, twenty expensive lofts, each equipped with an elevator for a car. Definitely worth a look for car fans is the **Oldtimer center Bremen**. In glass workshops, timeless car classics are maintained, repaired and sold. The freely accessible passage in the heart of Speicher 1 features a display of over 50 classic cars. The Oldtimer center offers sometimes guided tours through the world of old automobiles.

www.schuppeneins.de

We follow the **Übersee-promenade** to the west. The promenade itself offers space not only for pedestrians, skaters and cyclists; it is also an important component of the city's **flood protection system**. 18 million Euros had to be spent to lift the flood protection line – necessary due to rising sea levels. At the same time, a lower promenade was also constructed, creating a path to stroll directly along the water.

Where the harbor basin joins the Weser, in addition to a series of waterfront apartments, the tallest residential building in the Überseestadt so far has emerged at 70 meters in height: the **Landmark Tower** (8). It is comprised of exclusive condominiums with a breathtaking view of the Weser river. The "Suites of the World" are, however, beyond the means of most people.

The Sky-Bar atop the tower is only available for private parties, but on the ground floor, the **RIVA** restaurant awaits guests with Mediterranean cuisine. The promenade now leads through the most western area of the Überseestadt, where above all, new apartments emerge. In 2011, the Überseestadt had only 288 inhabitants, in 2019 it will be well over 2,000 and by 2030 it will be just under 7,000.

The promenade follows new residential buildings to the **Molenturm** (9), an essential navigational landmark for the ship and boat traffic on the Weser. In earlier times, a tower guard guided arriving merchant ships, using a megaphone, into the harbor. The Molenturm, Inow named the »Mouse Tower« by the people of Bremen.

From here, there is a beautiful view of Bremen's legendary Gröpelingen district to the West: One recognizes **PIER 2**, a trendy and very popular venue for parties and other events here in Northern Germany. Beyond this, the century-old grain silo **Getreideverkehrsanlage** looms impressively in the distance. On weekends between May and October, an hourly **pedestrian and bicycle ferry** (10) connects the Molenturm with PIER 2 an the Lankenauer Höft.

www.weserfähre-bremen.de

In May 2019, a new city beach and recreation area called **Waller Sand** (11) was opened directly at the ferry dock – a beautiful summertime oasis overlooking the large water areas of the ports and the Weser. Originally, this was the entrance to the Europahafen, which was filled in to start the new urban development. In 1998, a stone embankment was built as flood protection. During eventual renovation of that embankment, the chance arose to turn the entire area into a beach park and thus create a special public space for the new inhabitants of Überseestadt. Bremen has also played a pioneering role here: the Waller Sand is a model project for future **flood protection** that incorporates such protection zones into urban areas, and makes for a fluid boundary between city and water. Where previously warning signs pointed

The Molenturm still functions today as a navigational landmark on the Weser

out the danger of the water's edge, now families can enjoy a picnic on the beach and children can romp among trees and in the water. However, swimming is still not possible due to shipping traffic.

Waller Sand to Speicher 11

We now leave the westernmost tip of the Überseestadt and ride east – no longer along the water. Soon, we arrive at the **Überseepark** (12), a 25,000 m^2 park intended to meet the leisure interests of children and adolescents. With the help of the association Sportgarten e.V., a popular skating facility has been created here: on nice days, young people from all around Bremen come to perform acrobatic tricks, play football or just to chill in the open air

Passing some new apartment blocks you can see the great halls of the **wholesale market** (13), where Bremen's restaurants, weekly markets and retailers get their supply of food, flowers and specialties from all over the world.

The heart of the Überseestadt: Speicher 11

At the end of that area, we turn left and pasarrive at the 400-meter-long former warehouse **Speicher 11** (14) – built in 1912 – now housing the School of Fine Arts and other institutions. Not only university studies are offered there but also organizes the HFK several hundred cultural and art events every year, making it an important venue for the city life.
Info: www.hfk-bremen.de

In Speicher 11 you will also find the small but interesting **Hafenmuseum** (harbor museum), with interactive items and interesting photo and film materials from the harbor's history. How does cotton feel? How does fishmeal smell? How heavy is a coffee bag? Here, the social history of the Bremen harbor comes to life for children and adults alike.
The harbor museum leads to the **Überseestadt information center**. Since 2004, it has informed visitors on the development of the district. A highlight is the scale model of the Überseestadt, which is continually updated, offering an up-to-date bird's eye perspective.

Hafenmuseum (Harbor museum)
Speicher 11, Am Speicher 11 1, Tel. 3038279, Tue-Sun 11am - 6pm,
www.hafenmuseum-speicherelf.de

Also at the Speicher 11 is the **Bremen Center for Urban Culture** (Bremer Zentrum für Baukultur, named »b.zb«) located. Since 2004, the team has presented exhibitions, workshops, lectures and discussion events on current issues around urban architecture, such as the lecture series »Approaches to Building Culture«. The archive features planning documents for public and private projects, and in their extensive library not only architecture students find numerous treasures.
www.bzb-bremen.de

Opposite the Speicher XI, in the former stevedores offices, one can play minigolf under a black light. The ambience of the **SchwarzLichtHof** reminds of a time when goods were still being shipped through the harbor. The minigolf course has a harbor theme – players make their

View in the SCHWARZLICHT minigolf

way through an 18-hole course amidst barrels, packing cases and palettes, all under black lightning. A few steps further on, the creators have developed another original leisure attraction: the **HafenRummel** (harbor hustle and bustle) with 1950s-style fairground games. At 12 stations, skill, speed and luck are necessary to reach the goal. A really intresting way to lay his head down for the night is renting one of the old caravans at **HafenTraum,** an indoor hostelcamp which offers space for 33 sleepers. Have a look at their websites for detailed info.
www.ueberhafen.de
www.hafentraum.de
www.hafenrummel.de,
www.schwarzlichthof.de

From the square in front of the Speicher XI, we come directly to the **Timber and Factory Harbor** (15), which today handles primarily coffee and livestock feed. Here, too, we come upon a pioneer in the conversion of the old port areas: When the Überseestadt was just a vision, a creative agency settled into the former **port fire station** of red bricks, and continues to do interdisciplinary there. On the ground floor, you will find the terrace restaurant »Zur Feuerwache« in the historical buildings occupied formerly by harbor fire department. Directly on the harbor basin, it offers a unique view and beautiful sunsets.
A little further along the pier, the **Lloyd Caffee** Ltd. roastery and coffee shop(16) welcomes its guests. This coffee company moved into the former HAG factory in 2009. Here you can follow roasting master Christian Ritschel at work, and witness the entire roasting process while tasting different coffees in his coffee shop.
Finishing this tour bike tour on the small wooden sun terrace of the Lloyd coffee shop with some refreshing drinks or coffees is recommended.
Info: www.lloyd-caffee.de

Excursions

The Übersee-Museum, located right next to the central station

The Übersee-Museum

In the immediate vicinity of the Central Train Station, a Bremen institution awaits visitors: the **Übersee-Museum** (Overseas-Museum). It is rare to find a school child in Bremen who is not astounded by the Übersee-Museum with its plethora of exotic curiosities donated by Bremen researchers, explorers, and merchants over the century of the museum's existence. Since 2002, successive sections of the permanent collection have been fundamentally re-worked and modernized. Careful use of interactive media, sound and image stations designed for different age groups, and the placement of old exhibits into new contexts, have transformed the old institution into a place to confront today's world. Exhibits focus on such issues as migration, climate change, communication, and global economics. The history of colonialization and human rights are also central topics in various exhibits. Every other Friday: Night at the museum. With flashlights, guests explore exhibits from Oceania, Asia or Africa. The museum has established itself as a place of learning outside of school, offering numerous projects for children and young people from Bremen and beyond. Additionally, the Übersee Museum gives further insight into Bremen's merchant and marine history. Curious visitors will find facsimiles of old warehouses and store rooms, as well as learning about the sophisticated logistic systems of the earlier Bremen merchants of the Hanseatic League up to the 19th Century. Information on the Weser and its ecology, as well as its significance for the entire region, is also part of the museum's permanent exhibition.

Übersee-Museum
Bahnhofsplatz 13, Tel. 160380,
Tue–Fri. 9am–5pm, Sat–Sun
10am–5pm,
www.uebersee-museum.de

Unique Landscape: the Bürgerpark

From the »Bürgerweide« just behind the Central Station, eastward beyond the ÖVB Arena, lies the **Bürgerpark** (See detailed map inside cover). Your first glimpse of the park, however, will be a large baroque style pool, the Hollersee, reflecting the large dome of the Park Hotel, one of Bremen's best hotels. Finally, beyond the hotel, the park (often called the city's »green lung«) begins. Here the view opens onto wide meadows and a far-off perspective of the **Meierei**, which lies almost at the other end of the 200 hectare area.

Like the Wallanlagen (Battlement Park), the Bürgerpark was conceived as a landscape garden some 130 years ago. Amidst the calculated visual axes, waterways, lakes, bridges, both lawn and »wild« meadows, old trees, monuments and wrought iron benches, the natural and the artistic blend seamlessly; each can find something to his own taste. In the summer, the lawns are dotted with sun-worshippers, families and play groups find their way to one of the several playgrounds, walkers pause to rest on one of the historic benches, and at the Marcus Fountain, the »boule« players meet. But beyond these casual visitors, bird-watchers, herbologists and moody romanticists love to spend any time of year here. The autumn and spring are special times of wind and weather, when the play of color and light is especially fine. Look for the »Lyrical Path,« (the first of the poetry »stations« is at the Park Hotel) and follow the path, enjoying the lines (mostly in German) on flower and woodland, from Wilhelm Busch to Theodor Fontane, at each station.

Not far from the Melchers Bridge you will find a little **zoo** with sheep, chickens, goats, and donkeys along with a few exotic surprises – llamas, mufflons, and peacocks, amongst others. Nearby is the **Emmasee**, named for the Duchess Emma who was responsible for giving Bremen the land for this park. On the lake is a traditional café with a terrace overlooking the water. For a good meal and a wonderful view the Café Emma am See is unbeatable.

Emma am See

Family restaurant featuring contemporary German cuisine, Tel. 84138470, Tue–Sun 9am – 11pm, www.emma-am-see.de

The café Emma Am See, seems to float over the water

A party of boaters in the Bürgerpark

On the opposite side of the Emmasee is a boat rental office. The extensive waterways circle through the entire park, and a leisurely row is one of the most pleasant ways to see the whole thing. The Meierei, that Swiss gingerbread house you saw at a great distance when you first entered the park, is also worth a visit. It was built in 1880 to house a model dairy for an exhibition. Nowadays, the Meierei is the place for a special meal in the evening, or for a snack or coffee and cake in the afternoon. On the beautiful terrace, you can look back toward the far-off Park Hotel where you started and, if you have sharp eyes, you might also be able to see the spires of the cathedral all the way back at the »Domshof.«

At the north end of the park is the **Waldbühne** (The Forest Stage), called such, because every Sunday in the summer, a late morning jazz concert takes place. But on any other day, as well, it's a peaceful, pleasant oasis for a beer and a snack in the beergarden.

Divided from the Bürgerpark by railway tracks, yet part of it, the **Stadtwald** (city forest) is a paradise for joggers and athletes, who regularly seek out the »finnbahn« (running and fitness track) through the woods. The Stadtwald has always been just a bit less cultivated than the Bürgerpark. Appropriately, it is the home of the Waldkindergarten (Kindergarten in the Woods), so if on some misty autumn morning you should be surprised by a troup of smudged and rollicking little people on the path, don't worry – they belong here, at least during the time from 8:00 to noon.

Yet further to the north, the Stadtwald borders to the Unisee – a much-loved and in summer times crowded lake, so pack your bathing suit!

Bürgerpark

All Information on events, flora and fauna, features such as benches or bridges, is available at:
www.buergerpark.de

Universum Bremen: Science you can touch

Is it a huge shining metallic oyster, or is it a whale? Maybe a spaceship? The futuristic design by Bremen architect Thomas Klumpp is astonishing on its own. 40,000 stainless steel shingles sparkle in the sun and make the **Universum Bremen** visible from afar. With its silver-covered, whale-shaped perma-

nent exhibition building, the interactive museum opened in September 2000 is not only an integral part and a landmark of Bremen's cityscape, but also a magnet for visitors: every year over 200,000 inquisitive guests visit the city's most popular leisure and cultural center..
Inside the **»Silver Whale«**, young and old go on an exciting research trip and immerse themselves with all senses in the world of science. Around 250 interactive objects from the fields of technology, mankind and nature are waiting to be tried out. An eight-meter long ball track provides fascinating moments when up to ten billiard balls rotate directly above the heads of the observers. What kind of silhouettes are created when several light sources hit a body at the same time? Other spectacular attractions include the artificial tornado, quiet time in a completely darkened room, where you can discover your tactile sense, and the earthquake simulator, where a sofa shakes the walls at the touch of a button.
Regularly changing special exhibitions and daily science shows with astounding experiments complete the diverse range. In addition, the visit to the Universum is rounded off with a spacious outdoor area, the **Discovery Park**. On an area of 5,000 square meters, research is carried out outdoors - for example, on the lunar jumper, which raises one to four meters in height, or numerous water experiments – perfect for children on hot summer days! At the center is the 27-meter-high »tower of the air«, where experiments with wind and air can be performed. From the top of the tower, you can even see the spires of the cathedral in the city center on a clear day.
With its successful combination of information and fun, the Universum is a pleasure for adults and children alike. A must for every visit to Bremen! However, be sure to give yourself enough time for the experience – or plan more than one visit.

Universum Bremen
Wiener Straße 1a, Tel. 33460, Mon - Fri: 9am – 6pm, Sat/Sun and public holidays: 10am – 6pm, www.universum-bremen.de

The mysterious oyster: the Universum

The legendary airplane »Bremen« in an Airport-Showroom

Into Space with Astrium

Bremen is an important location for the air and space industry. Parts of the Ariane Rocket are built here, as well as space vehicles such as the »Space Hopper« a 20-ton transporter ATV designed to bring essential supplies to the International Space Station. For insight into Bremen's space industry, the BTZ (Bremen Technology Center) offers a tour of **Astrium**.

EADS Astrium

Visitors will receive a glimpse into the modern space industry with the help of expert guides. Tours Sat 2pm and 4pm, lasting approx. 2 hours. Possible last minute cancellations due to company needs. Booking exclusively through BTZ, Tel. 3080010, www.bremen-tourismus.de.

The »Bremen« at the Bremen Airport may be viewed 10am–6pm

The Scent of the Ocean in Vegesack

Vegesack lies nearly 20 kilometers to the north of Bremen's city center on the A27 by car, by train from the central train station, or along the Weser by boat. To this day Vegesack is Bremen's most maritime suburb, proven yearly at the »Hafenfest,« which takes place at the old harbor. The festival is pure maritime: traditional ships and sailing boats, captains and cadets, shanties and hornpipes. From the cafés and restaurants on the water, you have a fine view of the Weser. The **training ship »Deutschland«**, a 70-meter historic ship on which enlisted personnel are still trained, is also moored there along the Weser. You can board the ship for a tour, or even arrange to have your wedding there.

Schulschiff Deutschland
Zum Alten Speicher 15,
Tel. 6587373, Mon–Fri 10am–6pm,
www.schulschiff-deutschland.de

The ship »Deutschland« in Vegesack, where naval recruits learn their craft

Next, take the ferry from the harbor up the Weser to the **Strandlust**, a traditional continental restaurant and hotel. Beyond this, enjoy the **Stadtgarten** (City Garden) extending along the pleasant wharf.

Close by Vegesack lies Grohn, where you will find the **Jacobs University Bremen**, a prestigious private university attracting talented young people from all over the world. The beautiful, spacious campus is situated on the grounds of a former military base.

Jacobs University Bremen
Campus Ring 1, Tel. 20040,
www.jacobs-university.de
Info: www.vegesack.de

A Suburb of New York: Bremerhaven

In August, 2005, the largest hands-on museum in Europe on the theme of **emigration** opened in Bremerhaven. Directly next to the harbor, visitors can explore the 2,200 square meter space of the carefully arranged exhibits and form an idea of how it might have been 150 years ago, to leave home and travel through Bremen bound for the New World. Between 1830 and 1974, over seven million people began their overseas passage here.

Along with the permanent historical exhibition on emigration, the museum offers an extensive databank in its Fo-

Old semaphor at the entrance to the new harbor

rum Migration, with which visitors can do some family research on passengers who went through Bremen.
In 2012, the **Deutsches Auswandererhaus** (German Immigrant House) underwent an expansion. The exhibition now includes the lives and travails of immigrants to Germany starting in the 17th Century.
Bremerhaven has some striking new silhouettes on its horizon. This new ensemble of buildings is joined under the name, **Havenwelten**. The 148-meter tower of the ATLANTIC Hotel SAIL is prominent in the scenery of the old and new harbors. A trip to the visitor's deck of the hotel will, most literally, be the high point of your Bremerhaven visit.
The **Klimahaus** is a unique experience taking you around the world along the 8°E line of longitude beginning and ending in Bremerhaven. Over an area of 5000 square meters visitors witness first-hand the wonders of this world as they walk through the different climatic zones: hot and dry, subtropical-humid, and icy-polar. There are more than 100 interactive exhibits while innumerable background films and displays give insight into the interplay of nature, climate and human society. The many interviews gathered worldwide are certainly unique in the collection. They illustrate the fragility of culture and society in the global village, and how the stroke of a butterfly's wing can stir a Tsunami on the other side of the world.
For fans of all things nautical the **Deutsches Schiffahrtsmuseum** (German Naval Museum) allows visitors a glimpse into the 2000-year history of Northern European seafaring, including a locally-excavated shipping vessel from the Middle Ages.
For children, the **Zoo am Meer** (Zoo-on-the-Sea) is a wonderful attraction. It is small enough to be done on short legs, but big enough to offer good variety. The glass observation areas to the aquariums bring the penguins, sea-lions and polar bears (almost) close enough to touch as they swim by at the windows. The petting zoo includes rabbits and guinea pigs.
A stroll along the wharf, where the Weser meets the ocean, and a bus tour through the harbor, are a must on a trip to Bremerhaven.

Info: www.bremerhaven.de

Deutsches Auswandererhaus
Columbusstr. 65, 27568 Bremerhaven, Tel. 0471-902200, March–Oct. daily 10am–6pm, Nov.–Feb. daily. 10am – 5pm,

The German Emigrant Museum (Deutsche Auswandererhaus) in Bremerhaven: between 1830 and 1974, seven million people from all over Europe left for America and other countries through this port

www.dah-bremerhaven.de

Klimahaus® Bremerhaven 8 Ost
Am Längengrad 8, 27568 Bremerhaven, Tel. 0471 9020300, Apr.–Aug. 9am–7pm, Sat–Sun 10am–7pm, Sept.–March, daily, 10am–6pm, www.klimahaus-bremerhaven.de

Deutsches Schifffahrtsmuseum
Hans-Scharoun-Platz 1, 27568 Bremerhaven, Tel. 0471-482070, March–Oct. daily. 10am–6pm, Nov.–Feb. Tue–Sun., 10am-6pm, www.dsm.museum

Zoo am Meer
H.-H.-Meier-Str. 7, 27568 Bremerhaven, Tel. 0471-308410, Apr.–Sept. 9am–7pm, March–Oct., 9am–6pm, Nov.–Feb. 9am–4.30pm www.zoo-am-meer-bremerhaven.de

Birches and Brushes: Worpswede and Fischerhude

Around 1900, a number of artists fleeing the hectic materialism of the city, settled in **Worpswede**, a village then, secluded amidst inaccessible moorlands. Seeking to return to the roots of painting – light, color, and simple things – they found the wildly romantic scenery of Worpswede more than sufficient in all respects.
Today we associate Worpswede with artists such as Fritz Mackensen, Otto Modersohn, Fritz Overbeck and Hans am Ende, whose dark and melancholy landscape portraits have strongly influenced Northern Germany's image in painting. Reflecting different philosophical and artistic trends, however, were the socialist utopian Heinrich Vogeler, as well as modernist Paula Modersohn-Becker, sculptor Carla Westhoff and poet Rainer Maria Rilke, whose

Monument of Paula Becker-Modersohn in Worpswede

influences were also strongly manifested within the artist group. Worpswede is still an artist colony, though those living and working there today have long freed themselves from the direct influence of their predecessors.

Numerous galleries and museums have taken on the tasks of curating the old masters and presenting current artworks. Bremen sculptor Bernhard Hoetger's expressionistic building housing the **Große Kunstschau** now exhibitions the widest variety of the first Worpswede painters. Older works may also be seen in the former **residence** of Otto Modersohn and Paula Modersohn-Becker. The **Kunsthalle Friedrich Netzel** presents Worpswede works from all periods, while the **Alte Molkerei** is a venue for international works. Under the rubric »Masterplan Worpswede« you will find all of the museums in Worpswede listed. All of the houses have been renovated and, increasingly, the museums are coordinating their exhibitions and cooperating to re-work their materials.

Infos: www.worpswede-museen.de

Heinrich Vogeler restored and reconstructed the **Barkenhoff**, a gem among his early works. After the shock of the First World War, Vogeler became enamored of the radical left and made the place into an agricultural commune. Later, it served as a vacation resort for the children of impoverished urban workers. Nowadays, art exhibitions take place in the main building, and art students of the Barkenhoff Foundation work in the other buildings.The Heinrich Vogeler Collection may be viewed at **Haus im Schluh**.

The artists have had a hand in building nearly everything in Worpswede. In 1910 Heinrich Vogeler created the **Worpsweder Bahnhof**, in which today you will find an excellent restaurant and pub. The Kunstschau is not the only building that Hoetger built. He also constructed the **Kaffee Worpswede** next door – generally known in Worpswede as the Kaffee Verrückt, or »Crazy Coffee«.

Heinrich Vogeler's Barkenhoff

After all of the painted landscapes, don't forget to take a look at the real scenery. Though the **Teufelsmoor** has long lost its dark reputation for city-dwellers, it is still a unique natural landscape. A tour will make the history and culture of the area which inhabitants called »Dovelsmoor« or »Dead land,« more accessible.

This area of untillable and uninhabitable land was first systematically enclosed by Jürgen Christian Findorff (1720 – 1792) in the 18th century. After this time, peat moss, a valuable fuel for Bremen, was harvested in the extensive high moor between Bremervörde, Ritterhude and Fischerhude. A broad network of canals and streams then served as ways for the typical dark red-sailed peat barges bringing the peat to Bremen. Today, you can tour this peculiar and beautiful landscape on the canals in replicas of these barges.

Tourist-Information Worpswede
Bergstr. 13, 27726 Worpswede,
Tel.: 04792-935820,
www.worpswede-touristik.de,
info@worpswede-touristik.de
Torfkahn-trips
May - Oktober from Neu Helgoland
Worpswede, Tel. 04792-935820

Fischerhude is idyllically removed from the hectic whirl of Bremen, Lying on the small, meandering Wümme, also a tidal river, the village was home to some of the Worpswede artists. One of them, Otto Modersohn, lived here after his wife Paula Becker-Modersohn died. He liked the remote atmosphere of this tiny place and was working here until his death in 1943. Nowadays many visitors enjoy lots of garden cafés, small galeries, old farm houses and restaurants .

Otto Modersohn Museum
In der Bredenau 95, 28870 Ottersberg, Tel. 04293-328,
tgl. 10–18 Uhr
www.modersohn-museum.de
www.fischerhude.com

Aerial view on the City of Bremen

Travelinformation from A–Z

Travelinformation from A to Z

Area tel. code 0421 (international calls +49-421) unless otherwise indicated.

ADAC (German Auto Club) Towing Service

Tel. 0180-2222222, www.adac.de

Arrival

By car:
A1 north from the Ruhr area, or west from Hamburg, A27 north from Hanover or south from Bremerhaven.

By train:
Bremen is on the ICE line, IC trains available to all large cities. The main train station is in the city center. Travel information available from the Deutsche Bahn under the following number: 01800-599-6633
www.bahn.de

By air:
From the airport take the Tram No. 6 to the city center/central station (approx. 15 minutes).
Information: Tel. 55950,
www.airport-bremen.de

Tickets & Tourist Info

Bremer Touristik Zentrale (BTZ),
Service-Hotline: 3080010, Mon–Fri 8.30am–6pm, Sat 9.30am–1pm
IINFO: Central Train Station,
Mon–Fri 9am–6.30pm, Sat/Sun 9.30am–5pm
INFO: Böttcherstr. 4 / Marktplatz,
Mon–Fri 9.30am–6.30pm, Sat 9.30am–5pm, Sun 10am–4pm (during the christmas market Sat/Sun until 6.30pm)
The tourist information provides complete service: competent advice, brochures, all you need to know about sights, events, tickets, guided tours, town hall visits, hotel reservations, package holidays, river cruises, museums, tickets for events, souvenirs, and much more.
info@bremen-tourism.de
www.bremen-tourismus.de

Glocke, Domsheide 4/5,
Tel. 336699, Mon–Fri 10am–6pm, Sat 10am–3pm

Ticket Service Center TSC,
www.tsc.de

Biking

Bremen is a model city for bike-riders, with special bike lanes on nearly every street. To promote cycling, there is a bike-sharing system in Bremen called WK-Bike: At over 40 stations or freestanding in the city, nearly 500 bikes are available to registered customers around the clock. Check www.wk-bike.de, Hotline: 36713617
The Allgemeine Deutsche Fahrrad Club or »ADFC« (German Bike Club) Station and bike services are located next to the Central Station. For more athletic visitors, Bremen Tourist Center (www.btz.de) has prepared a series of suggestions for short bike tours, to the Teufelsmoor, the artist colony Worpswede, and Fischerhude. The ADFC and other agencies such as Hal Över (see Shipyards), offer tours into Bremen's surrounding countryside by boat and bike. Or you can easily

plan your own bike tours in the areas between the Elbe and Weser with ADFC Bike Tour Maps (1:150.000, Between the Elbe and Weser rivers / 1:750.000, Bremen and environs). An especially charming trip is by ship and/or bike along the Weser to Vegesack, then along the Lesum and the Wümme Rivers back through Blockland to the city.
Information also at the ADFC (German Bike Club), Main Train Station Square 14a, Tel. 79479511, open: Mon–Fri 10am –6pm, Sat 10am–2pm,
www.adfc-bremen.de
The Weser-Bikeway is also very popular. It starts in Hann. Münden and leads along the »Fairy Tale Route« over Hameln and Bremen to Bremerhaven. Information on the Weser-Bikeway-Hotline: Tel. 598290

Bistros, Bars and Restaurants

City center

1885 – Die Burger, Pelzerstr. 8, Tel. 3017888. Organic burgers on homemade buns
Alex Domshof, Domshof 16, Tel. 322670. Recommended for its wonderful view of the cathedral from the roof terrace
Alex Hanseatenhof, Hanseatenhof 1 , Tel. 1633980. Lively and delicious
Alte Gilde, Ansgaritorstr. 24, Tel. 171712. Cozy restaurant in the Guilds Hall in the center of Bremen
Beck's Bistro, Am Markt 9, Tel. 326553. Central location with a view on the City Hall
Bremer Ratskeller, Am Markt, Tel. 321676. The wine cellar is gathering place for locals and visitors alike. 600 excellent German wines available, the oldest wine cellar
D'Oro, Domsheide 6-8, Tel. 3366888. In the former cloister of the cathedral, a peaceful place in the center of the city, offering lunch and dinner menu
Friesenhof, Hinter dem Schütting 12–13, Tel. 3376666. Hearty food and fish dishes.
Gasthausbrauerei »Schüttinger«, Hinter dem Schütting 12–13, Tel. 3376633. A rustic micro-brewery offering german cuisine to enjoy with the house brews
Grashoff's Bistro, Contrescarpe 80, Tel. 14749, exklusive gourmet- and wine-bistro
Jackie Su, Langenstr. 10–12 Tel. 56518536. Fresh, delicious and inexpensive Asian cuisine in a clean-lined modern setting
Kaffeehaus Classico, Am Markt 17, Tel. 1784694. Restaurant and Café in a beautiful, classical atmosphere
Kaffee Mühle, Am Wall 212, Tel. 14466. In the Battlement Park (Wallanlagen) stands a century-old windmill. In the midst of this peaceful oasis you can enjoy food and drink
Kleiner Ratskeller, Hinter dem Schütting 11, Tel. 68492112. Good local cooking
L'Echalote, Hollerallee 99, Tel. 3789627. A gourmet restaurant located in the Hotel Maritim
Lemon Lounge Bremen, Am Wall 164, Tel. 5148855. Classic cocktails, whiskey and gin. In addition a wide range of workshops around the art of mixing is being offered
Muchos Más, Am Wall 135-136, Tel. 51705608. Authentic spanish ambience, spanish cuisine & bar

NOIR Coffee & Food Lounge, Langenstr. 6-8, Tel. 62062200. Coffee specialties & homemade snacks
Paddy's Pit, Bahnhofsplatz 5–7, Tel. 12310. Large, crowded Irish pub
Prego!, Knochenhauerstr. 3-4, Tel. 89785249. Pizza, pasta, bar
Spitzen Gebel, Hinter dem Schütting 1, Tel. 3306898. The oldest residential building in Bremen. From 1345–1948 it housed both tenants and businesses, starting in 1949 it became a locale for Bremen's merchants. The house speciality: »Sluk ut de Lamp«. Very small and famous
Ständige Vertretung im Flett, Böttcherstr. 3–5, Tel. 320995. Rheinish cult-pub with political flavor located in the historic Böttcherstraße
vapiano, Knochenhauerstr. 16–17, Tel. 168384. Good Italian food on a self-service model

Schlachte
Bolero Schlachte, Langenstr. 68, Tel. 707670. Mexican specialities and Cocktails
Camarillo, Schlachte 30, Tel. 1695454. Café, Bar and Restaurant
Luv, Schlachte 15–18, Tel. 1655599. Restaurant, café, bar
Osteria Restaurant, Schlachte 1, Tel. 3398207. Italian restaurant
Pannekoekschip »Admiral Nelson«, Schlachte/Anleger 1, Tel. 3649984. A »swash-buckling« experience young and old with over 100 varieties of pancakes from all over the world, unique setting and a view of the Weser river
Paulaner's, Schlachte 30, Tel. 1690691. Bavarian tavern, large beer garden right next to the Weser
Theaterschiff Bremen – Bühne 3, Tiefer 104/Anleger 4, Tel. 7908600. Bistro, restaurant and bar

Schnoor
Aioli, Schnoor 3–4, Tel. 323839. Spanish tapas bar
Beck's in'n Snoor, Schnoor 34–36, Tel. 323130. Comfortable restaurant; good, hearty food
Concordenhaus im Schnoor, Hinter der Holzpforte 2, Tel. 8980740. The restaurant for Bremen's specialties
Gasthof Kaiser Friedrich, Lange Wieren 13, Tel. 326429. Charming old pub in the Schnoor
Katzen-Café, Schnoor 38, Tel. 326621. Great fish in many different recipes
Kleiner Olymp, Hinter der Holzpforte 20, Tel. 326667. Fish and Northern German cuisine
Künstlerhaus Ausspann, Schnoor 1–2, Tel. 321124. A rustic culinary delight
Schröter's Leib & Seele, Schnoor 13, Tel. 326677. Mediterranean hors d'oeuvres and snacks in a pleasant atmosphere

In der Überseestadt
AL-DAR Syrisches Restaurant, Konsul-Smidt-Str. 26 (Schuppen Eins), Tel. 69686300. Fine Syrian restaurant with spectacular décor
Elisa, An der Reeperbahn 10 (opposite the Zollhaus), Tel. 47878087. Mediterranean restaurant
El Mundo, Konsul-Smidt-Str. 10a, Tel. 384010. Large selection of exotic dishes. Reservations recommended
Feuerwache, Waller Stieg 5, Tel. 3803808. Fine restaurant with a view of harbor activities
Hafencasino Truck Stop, Waller Stieg

6, Tel. 3962978. Taditional cuisine
Mekong Grill 2, Auf der Muggenburg 15, Tel. 57828762. Vietnamese cuisine
Port, Am Speicher XI, Tel. 619410. Delicious food in the atmosphere of the old harbor
RIVA, Konsul-Smidt-Str. 88 (Landmark Tower), Tel. 38039162. Delicious mediterranean cuisine on the bank of the Weser river
TASTE, Stephanitorsbollwerk 1 (Haus Lee), Tel. 17424558. Varied food creations.. Tasty spicy curries and also offerings for every tastes.

»Viertel«

Altes Fundamt, Auf der Kuhlen 1a, Tel. 7903939. The lunch specials come highly recommended. They're also organic
bellini, Vor dem Steintor 37, Tel. 7909726. Classic Italian cuisine where you get your money's worth
Platzhirsch, Ostertorsteinweg 50, Tel. 16980688. Rustic-cozy yet modern atmosphere, extensive menu
ChinChilla, Sielwall 4, Cocktailbar for night owls with an outdoor area
Don Carlos, Ostertorsteinweg 74, Tel. 705356. Excellent Spanish cuisine. They have a huge brunch buffet on Sundays. Reservations necessary
Gian Bastiano, Ostertorsteinweg 27, Tel. 69655100. Italian restaurant with a terrace and upper floors
Hegartys Irish Pub, Ostertorsteinweg 80, Tel. 701297. Pub mit Livemusik & großer Whiskykarte
Küche 13, Beim Steinernen Kreuz 13, Tel. 20824721. High quality regional cuisine in a small restaurant decorated in the style of the 1920s. Charming service, www.kueche13.de
Lei Bistro, Sielwall 55/57, Tel. 17511011. Delicious organic dishes such as soups, salads and razor-thin pizza
Litfass, Ostertorsteinweg 22, Tel. 703292. Bar with large outdoor service area. Concerts, readings, and football viewing
Loui & Jules, Vor dem Steintor 147, Tel. 79433533. Mediterranean restaurant with open kitchen
Lukullus, Vor dem Steintor 186, Tel. 76001. Has a 40-year tradition in the Steintor Quarter
Perlen & Primaten, Ostertorsteinweg 83. Trendy Cocktailbar
Rock & Wurst, Am Dobben 35, Tel. 67350189. Burger, steaks and rock 'n' roll
Tangente, Berliner Str. 41. Tel. 75222. Delicious Italian dishes made with organic ingredients
Theatro, Goetheplatz 1, Tel. 326080. A beloved meeting point that enjoys popularity beyond the theater-going crowd
Vengo, Ostertorsteinweg 91, Tel. 89785243. International vegan and vegetarian cuisine.

Cafés

At the city beach

Café Sand, Strandweg 106, Tel. 556011. In the summer, a small ferry will transport you back and forth from the Sielwall (Ostertor) to this favorite café. Everyone can be happy here, children can play in the sand and river while the adults enjoy a »Hefeweizen« beer

City

Café Stecker, Knochenhauerstr. 14,

Tel. 12593. Traditional café in the city
Creamlovers, Sögestr. 34, Tel. 17864800. Breakfast, snacks, italien ice cream und coffee specialties in the ambience of the golden 50's
Konditorei Knigge, Sögestr. 42–44, Tel. 13713. Not the famous author of etiquette books, but the baker, Wolfgang Knigge, invented his »Cappucine Torte« in 1883. The traditional Café Knigge still serves this and other wonderful sweets
Raths-Konditorei Stecker, Am Markt 11, Tel. 12593. Boulevard-café with view at the town hall, Roland and the St. Petri Cethedral. You will find more seats in the souterrain of the old patrician house on the west side of the marquet square

Schnoor

Café Tölke, Schnoor 23a, Tel. 324330. Surrounded by plush sofas and great tortes, you might feel you had been transported to a Vienna Coffee House
Teestübchen, Wüstestätte 1, Tel. 326091. The Teestübchen offers everything you need for a tea ceremony and great vegetarian dishes!

»Viertel«

Café Piano, Fehrfeld 64, Tel. 78546. Warm and cold meals, as well as daily specials. A favorite for breakfast
Engel Weincafé, Ostertorsteinweg 31, Tel. 69642390. A stylish mixture of cafe and wine specialty restaurant in the rooms of the old Engel Pharmacy
Harbour Coffee, Auf den Häfen 4, Tel. 3691000. Small and lovely, a heaven for coffee lovers and culture in a side street of the Viertel
NOON – Foyer Kleines Haus, Goeteplatz 1-3 (Courtyard), Tel. 326422. Perfect spot to unwind, eat and meet up amidst hustle and bustle of the theather
SOUL – vegan coffee bar, Am Dobben 65, Tel. 17531044. Vegan specialties & soulmade drinks
Wohnzimmer, Ostertorsteinweg 99, Tel. 1632064. A homey café with bunk beds and a video game corner

Along the Weser river

Bootshaus am Weserbogen, Auf dem Peterswerder 29, Tel. 437742. In the former clubhouse of the Bremen Sailing Club, everything is just right: Food & drink, stylish maritime ambience, picturesque location right on the small marina - view of the sunset included.
Café Ambiente, Osterdeich 69A, Tel. 4989508. Opened in 1929 as a non-alcoholic café between Viertel and Weser Stadium. Circular building with outdoor gastronomy, view of the Weser and a literature program.
Café Sand, Strandweg 106, Tel. 556011. A small ferry commutes between the Sielwall (Ostertor) and this popular café. Pretty famous among kids and their parents.

Camping

Camper Parking am Kuhhirten, Kuhirtenweg, 28201 Bremen, Tel. 0173-9850092, www.stellplatz-bremen.de Open all year, only 100 meters from the Weser, with a ferry for the city center within a few minutes walk
Hanse Camping am Stadtwaldsee, Hochschulring 1, 28359 Bremen, Tel. 30746825, www.hansecamping.de. Directly on the Stadtwaldsee (City Forest Lake), commonly known

Summer evening at Osterdeich, in the background Osterdeich-Beach

as the Unisee (University Lake), due to its proximity to University of Bremen. Terrace restaurant with a view of the lake, new toilet and wash facilities. By streetcar, from the university stop, the city center can be reached in approximately 15 minutes

Car Rental

Avis, Tel. 01805-217702,
www.avis.de
Europcar, Tel. 0180-58000,
www.europcar.de
Hertz, Tel. 01805-333535,
www.hertz.de
Sixt, Tel. 0180-5252525,
www.sixt.de

Childrens activities

Children will find lots to do in Bremen. Try ice-skating at Paradice in Walle or in winter at the Eissporthalle. In-line skating on various surfaces in summer. Most parts of the city have public swimming pools, inside and out. The Stadionbad is especially popular. Rowing on the canals of the Bürgerpark or enjoying the small zoo is lots of fun in the summer. A closer experience of the animals is possible at the »Neighbourhood Farms« (Stadtteilfarmen), which offer special programs during school vacations. At the Zoo am Meer (Bremerhaven), you can stand nose to nose with a polar bear, In autumn, there is always Freimarkt. Small kids will be happiest at the »Kleine Freimarkt« on the Marktplatz. Two theaters offer special programs for children: the MOKS Theater behind the Schauspielhaus and the Theaterkontor in the Schildstraße.
The Universum Bremen is appropriate for children starting at around 8 years old. Also exciting is a trip to the Übersee-Museum (Overseas Museum). The Klimahaus in Bremerhaven is also highly recommended.
The Olbersplanetarium offers a children's program almost daily. On the

visitors' terrace of the Bremen Airport, you can watch the planes come and go, or out in the Überseestade, the freighters, as you picnic on the river. On the Schlachte, the Pfannkuchen Ship »Admiral Nelson« should be a hit with the young ones, the free booklet »KinderZeit« (Kids' Time) announces numerous activities available during any given month. To let the kids tire themselves out on a rainy day, LEOS Spieleparadies (Play Paradise) at the Weserpark in Osterholz or the Linie 7, offering boulders and climbing possibilities (www.linie7.com). Finally the »Spiel and Sport Garden« near the Weser Stadium is wonderful fro athletic children and teens.
All events for children may be found in the monthly publication, »Kinder Zeit,« available free practically everywhere. www.kinderzeitung.de
Information is also available at www.bremen.de or in the free »Mix« magazine with event calendar, also available for free.

Cinemas

Atlantis, Böttcherstr. 4, Tel. 792550,
Gondel, Schwachhauser Heerstr. 207, Tel. 792550
Schauburg, Vor dem Steintor 114, Tel. 792550
Bremen's Art Film Theaters: Information under www.bremerfilmkunsttheater.de
Cinema im Ostertor, Ostertorsteinweg 105, Tel. 700914
Cinemaxx, Breitenweg 27, Tel. 040-80806969, www.cinemaxx.de
Kino City 46 / Kommunalkino Bremen, Birkenstr. 1, Tel. 95799290, www.city46.de. See movies in original language!

Cruises

The shipyard Hal Över offers many thematic cruises along with its series of traditional trips. The program is available on the Martini Quay, at the information stands of the Bremen Tourist Center or directly at Hal Över.
Weser and Harbor Tours:
Hal Över, Schlachte 2, Tel. 338989, www.hal-oever.de
The Turf-barges »Jan van Moor«, »Jan von Findorff« and »Jan von Bremen« can be chartered via the following email address: torfkaehne@bras-bremen.de

Emergency Numbers

Police, Tel. 110
Fire Department, Tel. 112
Emergency Medical Services, Tel. 19292
Emergency Medical Services for Children, Tel. 3404444
Dental Emergencies, Tel. 12233 (9am – 12am)
Women's Shelter, Tel. 349573

Event Venues

Congress Centrum Bremen (CCB), Maritim Hotel, Hollerallee 99, Tel. 37890, www.maritim.de
Die Glocke, Domsheide 4 – 5, Ticketservice Tel. 336699. Traditional Bremen concert hall.
ENERGIELEITZENTRALE, Am Speicher XI 11, 28217 Bremen, Tel. 2787946, www.energieleitzentrale.de
Haus der Wissenschaft, Sandstr. 4 – 5, Tel. 21869500, www.hausderwissenschaft.de
Kulturzentrum Lagerhaus, Schildstraße 12 – 19, Tel. 70100070, www.kulturzentrum-lagerhaus.de
Restaurant area, concerts, events, in

particular those of environmental or cultural interest

Kulturzentrum Schlachthof, Findorffstr. 51, Tel. 377750, www.schlachthof-bremen.de
Center for an alternative cultural scene in the former boiler room of Bremen's slaughterhouse. Avant garde theater, rock and punk, ethnic music and ambitious art and political projects

Lila Eule, Bernhardstr. 10, Tel. 7940664. The the bedrock of the Bremen student discos. Students today dance where their parents, and such political luminaries as Rudi Dutschke, danced in the '60s and '70s.

Modernes, Neustadtswall 28, Tel. 505553, www.modernes.de Bremen's most popular party and disco club.

ÖVB Arena, Findorffstr 101, Tel. 35050, www.oevb-arena-com
Up to 14,000 spectators can be accommodated in the hall of the Bremen Arena (former Stadthalle). Shows and conventions, large concerts, equestrian events, and the Six-Day Bike Race, take place here.

Pier 2, Gröpelinger Fährweg 6, www.pier2.de, Tel. 6918181. In Gröpelingen, Pier 2 is located in a former production hall of the traditional Bremen shipyard »A.G.Weser,« lending it an atmosphere of the old Bremen harbor. Pier 2 offers concerts, musicals and parties.

Schwankhalle, Buntentorsteinweg 112, Tel. 700141, www.schwankhalle.de. Modern event center for theater, dance and music.

St. Petri Dom, Sandstr. 10–12, Tel. 365040, www.stpetridom.de
Popular place for organ, choir, and chamber music concerts.

How to Find Out about Current Activities

All notable events in Bremen are listed not only in the daily newspaper, but also in the generally available (and free) city guide MIX (www.mix-online.de). The official Bremen portal, www.bremen.de, is also a good source for a well-organized daily listing of activities.

Information

BTZ Information Centers can be found at the following locations: Central Station, Mon–Fri 9–19:00, Sat/Sun 9:30–17:00.
Langenstraße / Marktplatz, Mon–Fri 10–18:00, Sat/Sun 10–16:00
Current brochures are available in these offices and both events and sightseeing tours can be booked here. Further information about hotels, etc., can also be obtained here.
Bremer Touristik Zentrale (BTZ), Findorffstr. 105, 28215 Bremen, Service-Hotline 01805-101030, (Hotel bookings, Events, City Bus Tours etc.), www.bremen-tourism.de, Information also available at:
www.bremen.de
www.bremen.de
www.bremerhaven.de
www.bremen-tourismus.de
www.schnoor-in-bremen.de
www.seestadtbremerhaven.de
www.vegesack.de
www.ueberseestadt.de

Galeries

The Northwest German art magazine »artist« has a monthly map of art events and a full catalogue of galleries and current exhibits.
www.artist-kunstmagazin.de

Guided Tours & Walks

The BTZ (Bremen Tourist Center) has an extensive program of guided tours and walks, of which we mention only a few: More information and inquiries: Tel. 3080010 www.bremen-tourismus.de

Daily walking tour of the city
From Jan.-April, on Sat at 1.30pm; May-Dec, daily 1.30pm, approx. 2 hours. From Jan.-April there will be a tour in German / English at 2 pm. Meeting point: on the right side in front of the Tourist-Information / Glockenspiel House in Böttcherstr. 4.

BCity Tours

By bus: Daily 11am and 12.30pm, length 80–90 minutes. Meeting point at 11am: Central Station Bus Terminal, Lane L.. Meeting point at 12.30pm, Domsheide tram stop 7, just in front of the Glocke Concert Hall.

Stadtmusikanten-Express: with the red-white electric train in the style of a locomotive through the city center (daily from 10.30am, several times a day, approx. 50 minutes) or the Überseestadt (daily 1.30pm, approx. 80 minutes) Experience the tourist attractions up close. Meeting point in front the Kontorhaus on marquet square/ corner Langenstr.)

Audioguide-Tour: Individual audio walk tour for adults and children through the city center and old town of Bremen. Available as download in various languages under www.bremen-tourism.de

Rathaus (City Hall) Tour

Mon–Sat at 4pm, Sun 12pm. (changes possible, no tours possible at senate receptions or events, for further information please contact the BTZ), length approx. 1 hour, meeting point at the Town Hall Entrance nearest the Cathedral, next to the statue of the knight on horseback (small door on the left, next to the display case).

Ratskeller Tour
Jan-Nov Fridays 4.30pm, length approx. 1 hour: Meeting point: on right side of Tourist-Information/Haus des Glockenspiels (Glockenspiel house) in the Böttcherstraße 4

Space Tour

Sat 2pm and 4pm, Length approx 2 hours, detailed info upon request

Bremen's Nightwatch

In recent years, guests and tourists have been able to take an evening tour with a traditional night watchman. While the good people of Bremen are "sleeping", the night watchman offers an entertaining journey through the Bremen of a bygone era as he does his rounds: follow him on his tour of the old quarter by night. Bookable via StattReisen, Tel. 4305656

The BTZ offers a variety of guided tours and walks of the city for groups (also with specific themes or subjects), guided pub tours and dinner tours can be arranged upon request! Various volunteer organizations also offer special tours to other locations.

Brewery Tour

If you love craft beers and want to experience the brewing craft up close, you can do so at Union Brewery Bremen. Craft beers from Bremen, brewery tour, beer seminars and much more are offered here. Next door the Union-Braugasthaus awaits you with snacks and food: Union Brauerei Bremen, Theodorstr. 13, Tel. 8982160, www.brauerei-bremen.de

Harbor tour

Kultur Vor Ort e.V., in cooperation with the Hafenmuseum in the Speicher XI, Kulturhaus Walle and Kulturhaus Pusdorf, offers a discovery tour through the ports of Bremen and the (otherwise inaccessible) port handling behind the lock. On board, you will learn interesting and entertaining facts about the history, the current activities and perspectives in the southernmost seaport of Germany. Dates and booking via shipping company Hal Över, Tel. 338989, Meeting point: Martini Pier (Martinianleger). Preregistration is preferred.
www.kultur-vor-ort.com

Hotels

The following selection is limited to Hotels and Bed/Breakfasts in central Bremen. For further choices and reservations, contact the Bremen Tourist Center (BTZ), Tel. 3080010, www.bremen-tourismus.de/hotels
Atlantic Grand Hotel Bremen****, Bredenstr. 2, Tel. 620620
Atlantic Hotel Universum****, Wiener Str. 4, Tel. 24670, www.atlantic-hotels.de
B&B Hotel Bremen**, Findorffstr. 28-32, Tel. 619580
Best Western Hotel Bremen City***, Bahnhofstr. 8, Tel. 30870, www.best-western.de
Best Western Hotel Zur Post****, Bahnhofsplatz 11, Tel. 30590, www.bestwestern.de
City-Hotel Bremen**, An der Weide 18–19, Tel. 3648052, www.city-hotel-bremen.de
Designhotel ÜberFluss****, Langenstr. 72, Tel. 322860, www.hotel-ueberfluss.com
HafenTraum**, Indoor Hostel Camp, Cuxhavener Str. 7,Tel: 3038958. www.hafentraum.de
H+Hotel Bremen***, Wachtstr. 27-29, Tel. 36010, www.h-hotels.com
Hochzeitshaus****, Wüste Stätte 5, Tel. 0176-57849591, www.hochzeitshaus-bremen.de
Hotel Am Hillmannplatz Nr. 1**, Hillmannplatz 1, Tel. 13258, www.am-hillmannplatz.de
Hotel Buthmann**, Löningstr. 29, Tel. 2238057, www.hotel-buthmann.de
Hotel Hanseatic**, Glockengang 4, Tel. 325435, www.hotel-hanseatic-bremen.de
Hotel Haus Bremen**, Verdener Str. 47, Tel. 4327210, www.hotel-haus-garni.de
Hotel Heinisch*, Wachmannstr. 26, Tel. 342925, www.hotelheinisch.de
Hotel Lichtsinn ***, Rembertistr. 11, Tel. 368070, www.hotel-lichtsinn.de
Hotelschiff »Perle«, Schlachteanleger 3a, Tel. 33659850, www.hotelschiff-perle-bremen.de
Hotel Stadt Bremen***, Heinkenstr. 3-5, Tel. 949410, www.hotel-stadt-bremen-garni.de
Ibis Bremen Centrum**, Rembertiring 51, Tel. 36970, www.ibishotel.com
Ibis Styles Bremen Altstadt**, Faulenstr. 45, Tel. 30480, www.accorhotels.com
INNSIDE Bremen****, Sternentor 6, Tel. 24270, www.innside.de
InterCityHotel Bremen****, Bahnhofs-

platz 17-18, Tel. 16030
Maritim Hotel und Congress-Centrum****, Hollerallee 99, Tel. 37890, www.maritim.de
Courtyard by Marriot Bremen****, Theodor-Heuss-Allee 2, Tel. 696400, www.courtyardbremen.de
Monopol Boutique Hotel***, Slevogtstr. 23, Tel. 67319580, www.monopol-bremen.de
Munte am Stadtwald****, Parkallee 299, Tel. 22020, www.hotel-munte.de.
Park Hotel Dorint*****, Im Bürgerpark, Tel. 34080, www.park-hotel-bremen.de
Prizeotel Bremen City, Theodor-Heuss-Allee 12, Tel. 59499401, www.prizeotel.com
Radisson Blu****, Böttcherstr. 2, Tel. 36960, www.radissonblu.com
Ramada-Treff Überseehotel Bremen***, Wachtstr. 27–29, Tel. 36010, www.ramada.de
Residence***, Hohenlohestr. 42, Tel. 348710, www.HotelResidence.de
Star Inn Hotel Bremen Colum-bus***, Bahnhofsplatz 5-7, Tel. 30120, www.starinnhotels.com
Steigenberger Hotel Bremen****, Am Weser Terminal 6, Tel. 478370, www.steigenberger.com
Swissôtel Bremen*****, Hillmannplatz, Tel. 620000, www.swissotel.com
Townside Hostel, Am Dobben 62, Tel. 78015, www.townside-hostel.de. Located in the Ostertor/Steintor, one of Bremen's most popular quarters.
Townside Hostel Bremen, Am Dobben 62, Tel. 78015, www.townside-hostel.de
Turmhotel Weserblick***, Osterdeich 53, Tel. 7903054, www.hotelgruppe-kelber.de
Mitwohnzentrale (Lodging Central), Humboldtstr. 28, Tel. 19445, Mon–Fri 10am–6pm, Sat 10am–1pm, www.bremen.homecompany.de

Lost and found

Fundamt (Lost and Found), Tel. 361-10078 or 361-10081.
BSAG (Trams&Buses), Tel. 55967979, Mon–Fri 2pm–6pm.

Markets

Flower Market, Liebfrauenkirchhof, Mon–Sat 8–14:00
Bremer Kajenmarkt, Schlachte, Sa 10–16:00 (May–Sep.)
Findorff-Wochenmarkt (weekly market), between Neukirch- and Eickedorfer Str., every Tue & Thu 8am–1pm, Sat 8am–2pm
Flohmarkt (Flea market) Bürgerweide, Sun 7am–2pm www.breminale.de
Flohmarkt Hansa-Carré, Sun 7am–2pm www.breminale.de
Weserflohmarkt Schlachte, Sat 8am–2pm
Wochenmarkt (weekly market) Domshof, Mon–Fri 8am–2pm, Sat 8am–3pm

Museums

Cathedral Museum, St. Petri Cathedral, Tel. 3347142, Mon–Fri 10am–4.45pm, Sat 10am–1.30pm, Sun 2pm–4.45pm, Admission free!, www.stpetridom.de
Contains the most valuable objects found in the recent diggings in the cathedral. Medieval bishops' tombs, gold objects, textiles. The 1200-year

history of the cathedral and preceding structures is well-documented here. Outside of the cathedral, you will find the Bleikeller. Enter from the Glockengarten. The eight mummies preserved there for centuries are on view in open coffins. Open: April, May, October: Wed–Fri 10am–4.45pm, Sat. 10am–1.45pm, Sun 12pm–4.45pm; June–September: Mon–Fri 10am–5.45pm, Sat 10am–1.45pm; Sun 12pm–5.45pm

Focke-Museum, Schwachhauser Heerstr. 240, Tel. 6996000, Tue 10am–9pm, Wed–Sat 10am–5pm, Sun 10am-6pm, www.fockemuseum.de
The Focke Musuem, located out of the city center in a neighborhood of beautiful villas, is dedicated to showing Bremen's history. In the main building, permanent exhibits include paintings, sculptures and many models demonstrating Bremen history from its beginnings in 1200 and the building of the cathedral, to industrialization, to the shipyard crises of the 1980s. Regularly changing exhibits on various themes are also presented. The museum also has a repository of artefacts filling some 2000 square meters. In the historic houses next to the modern museum building are collections of objects and clothing representative of those used by prosperous citizens of the 18th to 20th centuries. Objects associated with seafaring, fishing and agriculture are also on exhibit. For a while now the museum has had a »Schaumagazin,« an exhibit of objects normally in storage. The historic house nearby exhibits a collection of furniture and clothing to show the lifestyle of the middle classes of the 18th–20th Centuries, as well as farm, nautical and fishing implements

GAK Gesellschaft für Aktuelle Kunst, Teerhof 21, Tel. 500897, Tue–Sun 11am–6pm, www.gak-bremen.de
The Society for Current Art provides a platform for contemporary art. Artists are invited from all over the world to participate in projects. The GAK exhibits not only in its own rooms, but also presents projects throughout the city

Gerhard-Marcks-Haus, Am Wall 208, Tel. 9897520, Tue–Sun 10am–6pm, Thu 10am-9pm, www.marcks.de
The Gerhard Marcks Haus is Bremen's museum for modern and contemporary sculpture. It is counted amongst the best sculpture museums both nationally and internationally, as well as being one of the most beautiful exhibition venues in Bremen. Not only are classic by Moore, Maillol or Giacometti shown, but also younger artists, demonstrating the vitality of the medium today. Over the past 40 years, the museum has developed a concept that intelligently combines the modern and traditional. As a research institution, the museum has established an international reputation

Kunsthalle Bremen, Am Wall 207, Tel. 329080, Wed–Sun 10am–5pm, Tue 10am–9pm, public tours: every Sun at 3pm, www.kunsthalle-bremen.de
Significant collection of European painting starting with the 15th Century. The collection emphasizes French and German art of the 19th and 20th Centuries, including Eugène Delacroix, Gustave Courbet, Wilhelm Leibl,

Max Liebermann, Max Slevogt, Lovis Corinth, and Max Beckmann. The Worpswede artists are expecially well-represented, including important works by Paula Modersohn-Becker The Copper Engraving Cabinet has one of the largest collections in Europe, including almost the entire works of Albrecht Dürer, but also works by Goya, Menzel, and Picasso. In the »Movement, Light Film, Video« exhibits, are works by artists such as John Cage, Peter Campus, Otto Piene, or Nam June Paik. With its special shows, the Kunsthalle regularly brings tens of thousands of visitors from all over Germany to Bremen.

Weserburg Museum für moderne Kunst, Teerhof 20, Tel. 598390, Tue - Sun 11am-6pm, www.weserburg.de
Collection of contemporary works, artfully exhibited in four re-constructed former warehouses. The museum sees itself as a neutral showplace for significant collections, some of which are permanently housed there, some only temporarily on exhibit. The varying emphases of the collections produce an appropriately paradoxical and thought-provoking overall image of the contemporary avant-garde

Paula Modersohn-Becker Museum und Ludwig Roselius Museum, Böttcherstr. 6–10, Tel. 3388222, Tue–Sun 11am–6pm, www.museen-boettcherstrasse.de
The Paula Modersohn-Becker Museum shows paintings, drawings, and graphic arts of that Worpswede artist. Some of Bernhard Hoetger's works are also shown there. The museum also regularly arranges special exhibits of contemporary artists. The Roselius-Haus is a collection of furnishings, art work and decorations typical of the patrician households of Old Bremen. The collection also contains the famed silver treasure of the »Company of the Black Heads Riga«

Übersee-Museum, Bahnhofsplatz 13, Tel. 16038101, Tue–Fri 9am–5pm, Sat+Sun 10am–5pm, www.uebersee-museum.de
The new special exhibits offers first-rate cultural and historical information and entertainment with a multi-media excursion to the South Seas and Asia. The museum's »old« departments, including anthropological, ecological, seafaring and trade exhibits from all over the world, are also still worth a visit. The museum presents Bremen's international trading history

Universum Bremen, Wiener Str. 1a, Tel. 33460, Mon–Fri 9am-6pm, Sat/Sun and on holidays 10am–6pm, www.universum-bremen.de
A futuristic structure next to the university houses this unique, well-founded learning & science museum. Universum offers interactive experiences and experiments with clear explanations on dozens of topics within its three areas of emphasis – universe, earth, and mankind. This is a great experience for children and adults alike. Very recommended

Wilhelm-Wagenfeld-Haus, Am Wall 209, Tel. 3388116, Tue 3pm–9pm, Wed–Sun 10am–6pm, www.wilhelm-wagenfeld-stiftung.de
The Wagenfeld Foundation and House are dedicated solely to modern industrial design. The work of Wilhelm Wagenfeld, a pioneer of German industrial design, is also exhibited here

Harbor Museum Speicher XI, Am

Speicher XI 1, 28217 Bremen, Tel. 3038279, Tue–Sun 11am–6pm, www.hafenmuseum-speicherelf.de
The creation of the harbors and presentation of the harbor trades are presented on an area of around 2000 square meters. This is a multi-sense exhibit: you can smell and touch the grains and wares, lift the sacks, load ships and tie knots. Models of freighters demonstrate the development of shipping between 1945 and the present day. Romantic ideas about seafaring and the hard realities on board collide, and the walkable floor model of the harbor area shows the development of the harbor economy in Bremen. An adjoining information center for the Überseestadt project reports on continuing developments in the area.
Wuseum - Werder Bremen Museum, Franz-Böhmert-Straße 1c, Tel. 434594350, Tue-Fri Noon-5pm (Jan-Feb 12-3pm), Sat-Sun + public holidays 12-3pm; Open on home match days, 3 hours to 1 hour before kick-off. www.werder.de
Start a green-white journey through time and experience almost 120 years of moving club history at the WUSEUM, the Werder Museum. From the beginnings and great successes to little stories that have made the SV Werder Bremen one of the popular and successful German football clubs. A must for all Werder fans but also interesting for all football fans.

Parking

The city's excellent parking system has 13 parking garages. The ParkTicket can be used within the city for all buses and trams from Monday to Saturday between 9:30 and 8:30 (max two adults and two children). The lines from Doventor to St. Jürgen Straße and Bürgerweide to the Weser River can be used with this ticket

Planetarium

Werderstr. 73, Tel. 408899300, www.planetarium.hs-bremen.de
With 12-channel light technology, the Olbers Planetarium presents a variety of entertaining, classical astronomy lectures under its artificial night sky

Public Transportation

Exploring Bremen is very easy without a car. Many streetcars and buses criss-cross the city. Major junctions include the Main Train Station and Domsheide. Furthermore, there are bike paths on virtually every street and all of the most important sites in the city center are within a walkable distance.
The BSAG (Trams&Buses) offers many special tickets for families and groups, for one day or longer. With the ErlebnisCard you can ride comfortably and cheap throughout the city and receive price reductions on tickets to many of the city's cultural institutions.
The buses labeled »N« (for »night«) will get you home safely, even into the early morning hours.
If you have any questions concerning bus, train or tickets, you can use the service-hotline (24hrs): Tel. 01805-826826, 0,12 e/Min. for calls on the landline from within Germany, www.bsag.de.

Shopping and Souvenirs

Sögestraße and Obernstraße are the traditional shopping streets of Bremen. On a comfortable stroll along the pedestrian street (Sögestraße) you might hear many a talented musician playing in front of the department stores, boutiques, traditional local stores, and the usual franchises there. In the last few years many shopping passages have been built. From the Domshof you can get to the luxury boutiques and elite bars of Domshof and Katharinen-Passages. Through the Lloyd-Passage adjoining Karstadt and other large department stores, you will reach the Ansgari Churchyard, and can continue to yet another shopping passage. Even the sidewalk before the elegant stores along Am Wall is now equipped with a glass roof to ensure rain-free window shopping.

Souvenirs and fine craft items are the main offerings in Böttcherstraße and the Schnoor. You will find everything there, from windsocks to jewelry, original teddy bears, Bremen chocolate, bottled ships, Schnoor cigars, famous tourist attractions worldwide – as paper models to build yourself, Christmas decorations year round, to the obligatory Bremen Town Musicians in all possible variations.

Flohmarkt (Flea Market) During summer, Saturdays 8am–2pm on the promenade of the Weser and Sundays 7am–2pm on the Bürgerweide and/or the Hansa Carrée.

The Wochenmarkt (a daily farmer's market) is located on the Domshof, Mon–Sat 8am–2pm. This is one of the best places in Bremen to find a wide variety of high quality fresh foods.

Sports

Eissporthalle Paradice, Waller Heerstr. 293a, Tel. 6198888, www.paradice.de

Bouldering and Climbing

Boulder Base Bremen, Hohweg 5 / Eingang Ingolstädter Straße, 28219 Bremen, Tel. 36564422, www.boulderbasebremen.de

Kletterbunker, Mählandstr. 35 Tel. 501124, www.der-bunker.net, nur im Sommerhalbjahr

Linie 7, Güterverkehrsbahnhof, Beim Handelsmuseum Tor 41–45, Tel. 57730327, www.linie7.com

Unterwegs – DAV Kletterzentrum Bremen, Robert-Hooke-Str. 19, 28359 Bremen, Tel. 51429053, www.kletterzentrum-bremen.de

Swimming

Es gibt zahlreiche Hallen-, Spaß- und Sportbäder. Für Sportler/innen besonders attraktiv das Sportbad Uni, für Kinder und Jugendliche das Stadionbad mit einer Steilrutsche für besonders Mutige. Alle Informationen über Hallenbäder unter www.bremer-baeder.de, Tel. 691370

German Bundesliga Football

Weser-Stadion, Franz-Böhmert-Str. 1, Tel. 696360, www.werder.de, www.weserstadion.de

Taxis

Frauen-Nacht-Taxi, special taxi for women during the night, Tel. 13334

Taxi-Roland, Tel. 14433

Taxi-Ruf, Tel. 14014 or 14141

Theater

Bremen Shakespeare Company, Theater am Leibnizplatz, Tel. 500222, www.shakespeare-company.com Mon–Fri 10am–2pm, 3–6pm, ticket sales: Tel. 500333, Tue–Sat 3–6pm. With radical new interpretations of Shakespeare the company has made a name for itself internationally. Just

Sports facilities in the »Überseepark«

like in Shakespeare's time the audience is absorbed into the dramas and comedies with panache and skill.
GOP-Varieté Bremen, Am Weser Terminal 4, Tel. 89898989
Junge Akteure, Brauhauskeller Theater Bremen Goetheplatz 1–3, Tel. 3653449, www.theaterbremen.de/jungeakteure
MOKS Theater am Bremer Theater, Goetheplatz 1–3, Tel. 3653449, www.theater-bremen.de
MOKS produces children's and young people's theater in conjunction with the Bremer Theater. They usually produce four pieces per season in the 99-seat Brauhaus Theater behind the Schauspielhaus Theater
Musical Theater am Richtweg, Richtweg 7–13, Tel. 3337590, www.musicaltheater-bremen.de
Tickets, Tel. 353637, www.tsc.de
Schwankhalle, Buntentorsteinweg 112, Tel. 700141, www.schwankhalle-bremen.de
Original and Guest Productions from the independent scene make this theater one of the most experimental and interesting stages in Bremen
Theater Bremen, Goetheplatz 1–3, Tel. 36530, ticket reservations Tel. 3653333, Mon–Fri 11am–6pm, Sat 11am–2pm, www.theater-bremen.de
A three-section house with several stages. In the area of dance the theater works in close cooperation with Oldenburg.
Theaterkontor Bremen, Schildstr. 21, Tel. 706582, 9–13:00, www.theaterkontor-bremen.de
The Theaterkontor Bremen produces remarkable adaptions of classical productions for children and adults on the smallest stage
Theaterschiff Bremen e.V., Tiefer 104, (ship is moored at the level of Tiefer Street, directly on the Weser), Tel. 7908600, www.theaterschiff-bremen.de
Located at Quay 4, the Theater Ship offers cabaret and comedy

Youth Hostel Bremen

Kalkstr. 6, Tel. 163820, www.jugendherberge.de/jh/bremen
Located in the city center, right next to the Weser river
HafenTraum**, Indoor Hostel Camp, Cuxhavener Str. 7,Tel: 3038958. www.hafentraum.de

Index

U

V

W

Children like to play with the pigs at the beginning of the shopping area »Sögestrasse«

Y

Z

Die Deutsche Bibliothek verzeichnet diese Publikation in der Deutschen Nationalbibliografie; detaillierte bibliografische Daten sind im Internet über http://dnb.ddb.de abrufbar.

Text: Lutz Liffers, Daniela Frankenstein, Johannes Eichwede
Cartography: Helmut P. Einfalt, Edition Temmen
Translation: Nancy Schrauf, Johannes Eichwede

Illustrations: Bremer Geschichtenhaus: 58; BTZ: 11, 13, 34, 44, 45, 49, 52, 54, 64, 74, 77, 78/79, 85; Deutsches Auswandererhaus/K. Riechers: 87; Die Glocke/Bollhorst: 34; Gerhard-Marcks-Haus: 64; © Hafenmuseum Speicher XI/F. Scheffka: 76; Jürgen Howaldt: 10d, 29, 35, 36, 37, 43, 46, 53, 55, 56, 57, 58, 80; © iStock.com/grahamheywood: cover; Kunsthalle/M. Gielen: 65; Torsten Krüger: 84; Lutz Liffers: 8u, 30, 33, 48, 81; Jochen Mönch: 14, 67, 82, 88, 89; Jürgen Nogai: 25; Ulrich Perrey: 59; Detmar Schmoll/Studio B: 4/5, 90/91; Thorsten Taubhorn: 60; Universum Bremen: 83; Verlagsarchiv: Cover, 2, 3, 7, 8b, 16/7, 18/9, 20, 23, 24, 26, 27, 28, 31, 38, 42, 43, 46u, 48/9, 50, 66, 73, 97, 107, 111; Wim Frankenstein: 10u, 17, 51, 75, 86; Ingo Wagner: 63; www.ueberhafen.de: 77; Zollhaus: 71

Sixth, updated edition 2019

Hohenlohestr. 21 – 28209 Bremen
Tel. 0421-34843-0 – Fax 0421-348094
info@edition-temmen.de – www.edition-temmen.de

Printed in the EU

ISBN 978-3-86108-920-9